PHILOSOPHY OF WRITING

ALSO AVAILABLE FROM BLOOMSBURY

Between Philosophy and Poetry, edited by Robert Burch and
Massimo Verdicchio
Why Write? Mark Edmundson
Philosophy and Literature in Times of Crises, Michael Mack

PHILOSOPHY OF WRITING

DAVID ARNDT

BLOOMSBURY ACADEMIC
LONDON • NEW YORK • OXFORD • NEW DELHI • SYDNEY

BLOOMSBURY ACADEMIC

Bloomsbury Publishing Plc, 50 Bedford Square, London, WC1B 3DP, UK
Bloomsbury Publishing Inc, 1359 Broadway, New York, NY 10018, USA
Bloomsbury Publishing Ireland, 29 Earlsfort Terrace, Dublin 2, D02 AY28, Ireland

BLOOMSBURY, BLOOMSBURY ACADEMIC and the Diana logo are trademarks of
Bloomsbury Publishing Plc

First published in Great Britain 2026
Reprinted 2026

Copyright © David Arndt, 2026

David Arndt has asserted her right under the Copyright, Designs and Patents Act, 1988, to be identified as Author of this work.

For legal purposes the Acknowledgments on p. vii constitute an extension of this copyright page.

Cover design: Ben Anslow

Cover image: Simone de Beauvoir on the day of the Prix Goncourt, Paris, 1954
(© RMN-Grand Palais / Gisele Freund / RMN-GP / Dist. Photo SCALA, Firenze)

This work is published open access subject to a Creative Commons Attribution-NonCommercial-NoDerivatives 4.0 International licence (CC BY-NC-ND 4.0, https://creativecommons.org/licenses/by-nc-nd/4.0/). You may re-use, distribute, and reproduce this work in any medium for non-commercial purposes, provided you give attribution to the copyright holder and the publisher and provide a link to the Creative Commons licence.

No part of this publication may be used or reproduced in any way for the training, development or operation of artificial intelligence (AI) technologies, including generative AI technologies. The rights holders expressly reserve this publication from the text and data mining exception as per Article 4(3) of the Digital Single Market Directive (EU) 2019/790.

Bloomsbury Publishing Plc does not have any control over, or responsibility for, any third-party websites referred to or in this book. All internet addresses given in this book were correct at the time of going to press. The author and publisher regret any inconvenience caused if addresses have changed or sites have ceased to exist, but can accept no responsibility for any such changes.

A catalogue record for this book is available from the British Library.

ISBN: HB: 978-1-3504-7390-4
PB: 978-1-3504-7389-8
ePDF: 978-1-3504-7391-1
eBook: 978-1-3504-7392-8

Typeset by Deanta Global Publishing Services, Chennai, India
Printed and bound in Great Britain

For product safety related questions contact productsafety@bloomsbury.com.

To find out more about our authors and books visit www.bloomsbury.com and sign up for our newsletters.

Of all writing, I love only what is written with blood.
Write with blood, and you will find that blood is spirit.

—FRIEDRICH NIETZSCHE

For Athena Kallista

CONTENTS

Questions

Why Write? 3

Language 7

Thinking 11

Truth 15

Goodness 23

Beauty 37

Inspiration 47

Wisdom 59

Writing as Meditation 65

Kinds of Thought

Ways of Thinking 75

Demonstration 77

Interpretation 81

Perspective 85

Narration 89

Kinds of Writing

Papers 95

Essays 97

Dialogues 101

Stories 107

Principles of Composition

Principles 129

Process 135

Outline 141

Argument 145

Questions 151

Examples 155

Quotations 157

Paragraphs 159

Sentences 165

Words 175

Afterword 181
Works Cited 186
Notes 194
Index 210

QUESTIONS

WHY WRITE?

Near the end of her life, Toni Morrison spoke of why she wrote: "I don't think I could have happily stayed here in the world if I did not have a way of thinking about it, which is what writing is for me.... It's a way of thinking."[1] These words seem strange—they challenge the most common views of writing today.

Writing is commonly seen in several ways: as a tool of communication; as a medium of self-expression; and as an imitation of living speech. But if we turn to the words of great thinkers, we find they articulate a different view of writing.

Epictetus said writing is a dialogue with oneself:

> "But wasn't Socrates a writer, and a prolific one at that?" Yes, but to what end? Since there wasn't always someone available whose ideas he could examine or who could examine Socrates' own in turn, sometimes he would test and examine himself, forever subjecting to scrutiny one assumption after another. That's the writing of a real philosopher.[2]

The point of writing, for Epictetus, is not just to communicate thoughts but to test and examine them. The practice of writing is also a way to make thoughts part of oneself, so that they are always ready to hand: "Have thoughts like these ready to hand by night and by day; write them, read them, make your conversation about them, communing with oneself." And writing is a way to cultivate the dispositions proper to a good life: serenity, gratitude, wonder, and joy: "That's the kind of attitude you need to cultivate if you would be a philosopher, the sort of sentiments you should write down every day and put into practice."

Nietzsche also tied writing to thinking: "To write better means at the same time to think better." But Nietzsche reversed the way this tie is usually conceived. It is not that we first have thoughts and then put them into words, so that clear thinking leads to good writing. The effort to write well itself lets us clarify, deepen, and refine our thinking. We tend to start writing not with fully formed thoughts, but with intuitions that are still inchoate and obscure, and we transform those intuitions into precise and illuminating thoughts through the long, slow, patient work of composition. Composition means finding words, constructing sentences, composing paragraphs, and working out the structure of a text. But it also means setting a tone, finding images, inventing turns of phrase, and sensing the rhythm and tempo of discourse—everything we point to with the word "style." Styles of writing, for Nietzsche, are not empty forms into which one pours the contents of one's mind. A style of writing puts into words a distinctive way of thought. So a care for thinking requires a care for written style. "To improve one's style—means to improve one's thoughts and nothing else."[3]

Hannah Arendt said something similar. For her, the point of writing was not just to communicate an understanding she had already achieved; it was to clarify, deepen, and refine her understanding. Not to incorporate the thoughts of others, but to work out an understanding of her own.

> When I am working, I am not interested in how my work might affect people . . . . What is important for me is to understand. For me, writing is a matter of seeking this understanding, part of the process of understanding . . . . What is important to me is the thought process itself.[4]

Writing for her was not just a way to convey to others what she already thought; it was a way to move toward her own understanding.

Michel Foucault also wrote in order to work out his thoughts.

> The books I write constitute an experience for me that I'd like to be as rich as possible. An experience is something you come out of changed. If I had to write a book to communicate what I have already thought, I'd never have the courage to begin it. I write because I don't yet know what to think about a subject that attracts my interest. In doing so, the book transforms me, changes what I think. As a consequence, each new work profoundly changes the terms of thinking which I had reached with the previous work. . . . When I write, I do

it above all to change myself and not to think the same thing as before.[5]

Writing here is an effort to transform not just *what* we think but the *terms* in which we think—to sharpen, refine, and redefine the language in which we understand the world.

This kind of writing changes us. In a way, it is similar to practices such as athletics for the body or meditation for the mind: just as the practice of physical exercise changes the body, so the practice of writing changes the soul. Gloria Anzaldúa made this point:

> Why am I compelled to write? . . . I write to record what others erase when I speak, to re-write the stories others have miswritten about me, about you. To become more intimate with myself and you. To discover myself, to preserve myself, to make myself. . . . The act of writing is the act of making soul.[6]

Writing for Anzaldúa is a matter not just of communication, or self-expression, or self-discovery, but also of self-formation and transformation.

It seems we learn a new care for writing when we start to see it for what it is. These six thinkers describe a kind of writing overlooked by common views: writing for them was not just a tool of communication, or a medium of self-expression, or a substitute for speaking, but also a path toward true understanding.

But how can writing be a path to understanding? What kind of understanding can be reached through work with language? What does the practice of writing reveal about the nature of language itself?

LANGUAGE

Writing is seen as a way to communicate when language itself is viewed as a tool of communication. But this view fails to see the place of language in human life. Every language articulates a common understanding of the world, in which things have sense and value for a community. To learn a language is to appropriate that common understanding and to move toward joining that community and entering its world. A child without language would not fully enter the human world or fully realize her potential as a human being. Language is not just a tool that humans have; it is in and through language that we become fully human.[1]

But the understanding we take from language is flawed in three ways:

1. It is *limited*. I can never fully appropriate the understanding implicit in my language—there are always words I don't know, senses I don't see, contexts I fail to grasp. No one masters a language completely. There is always more to learn.

2. It is *average*. I share with others an understanding that is, initially and for the most part, relatively shallow, confused, vague, simplistic, and crude.

3. It is *inauthentic*. The understanding implicit in language is not my *own*, one I have worked out through my own efforts, on the basis of my own thought and experience. It is an understanding I absorb from others in a passive and thoughtless way.

To move toward truth, we have to move in three directions:

First, from *ignorance* to *knowledge*. Knowledge brings thinking down to earth and away from vacuous abstractions. The more we know, the better we can understand.

Second, from an *average* toward a *genuine* understanding of things: from one that is relatively shallow, confused, vague, simplistic, and crude, toward one which is deep, clear, precise, complex, and refined.

Third, from an *inauthentic* toward a more *authentic* understanding of things: from an understanding we have thoughtlessly absorbed from others, toward an understanding that we have worked out through our own thought, in light of our own experiences, on the basis of our own reading, conversation, and reflection.[2]

Writing can be a path to greater understanding because the act of composing a text pushes us to think. William Zinsser used to say, "writing is thinking on paper."[3] Walter Kaufmann said, "Writing is thinking in slow motion."[4] Stanley Hauerwas wrote that "Writing is hard and difficult work because to write is to think. I do not have an idea and then find a way to express it. The expression is the idea. So I write because writing is the only way I know how to think."[5]

But to link writing and thinking clarifies nothing as long as the nature of thought remains unclear. We have to ask about thought itself: What is thinking? What does it mean to think?

THINKING

The most common concept of thinking today rests on several assumptions. Thinking aims at truth. The locus of truth is the proposition. Propositions are the core of belief. Beliefs are true when they correspond to reality. We can accept beliefs as true only if this correspondence can be verified. To verify a belief is to show the grounds for this acceptance: to show that beliefs have been reached through logically valid inferences; to show that they are based on clear and distinct evidence; and to show that they work pragmatically to explain and predict reality. The most basic assumption is that the aim of thought is knowledge, where knowledge is understood as justified true belief.

To think critically, in this view, is to suspend trust in our beliefs and to examine them objectively to see if they are logically valid, if they are grounded in clear and distinct evidence, and if they allow us to explain and predict phenomena in a reliable way. Critical thought in this sense is *demonstrative* in that it aims to prove a thesis.

This view of critical thinking underlies most composition courses. Students are asked to formulate a thesis and to offer evidence and arguments to show that it is true.

Where does this view of thinking come from? From what sphere of experience was it born? What are its limitations? And what are its blind spots?

The common concept of thinking is derived from the methods of modern science. Heidegger made this point in his "Letter on Humanism": "we conceive of thinking on the model of scientific knowledge and its research projects."[1] Scientific methods have been abstracted from their native sphere, generalized without limits, and read into the operations of the human mind. All thinking is viewed as a more or less crude version of scientific methods. This view is not scientific but *scientistic*—it is not based on evidence and argument but on the dogma that scientific research is the paradigm of all thought.[2]

This concept of critical thinking obscures other kinds of thought. It obscures *interpretive* thought, which aims to explicate and clarify the meaning of texts. It obscures *perspectival* thought, which explores the strengths, limits, and blind spots of various points of view. And it obscures the nature of *narrative* thought, which illuminates the possibilities of human existence by taking up and refining the stories in which we understand our lives. These other forms of thought underlie different kinds of writing, such as essays, dialogues, and stories.

We have to expand our view of thinking to include these other kinds of critical thought. Critical thought is not just a matter of suspending trust in beliefs in order to test their logical validity, their grounding in evidence, or their pragmatic utility. To think critically means to look for the strengths and limitations of the terms in which we understand ourselves and the world: the words with which we try to grasp what things are; the perspectives in which we are caught; and the stories in light of which we understand the possibilities of human existence.

Thinking aims at truth. Common concepts of truth underlie common concepts of thought. To reconceive the nature of thought, we also have to question the nature of truth. What are we aiming at when we aim at truth? In what senses can writing be true? What is truth?

TRUTH

Truth is usually seen as a matter of correspondence. Writing is true if it corresponds to reality. Theories are true if they fit the facts. A portrait is true if it reflects the person it portrays. Dialogue is true to life if it mimics the way people really speak. Stories are true if they represent the way things are. In each case, words are true if they correspond to reality in a complete and accurate way.

This is the most common concept of truth. It is implicit in our understanding of veracity in courts of law, verisimilitude in art, realism in fiction, and verification in science. The notion of truth as correspondence frames our view of the *veridical* dimension of writing—the power of written words to say what is true.

The concept of truth as correspondence is integral to the field of philosophy known as epistemology—the study of knowledge. But a few recent philosophers have pointed to the limits of epistemology as a field. Charles Taylor has argued that epistemology focuses on just one kind of understanding, which it takes to be knowledge in the strictest sense of the word, and that knowledge in this sense presupposes a level of understanding that precedes and eludes epistemological questions. The kind of knowledge studied by epistemology rests on a level of understanding that exceeds the grasp of epistemology's basic concepts: "This shows the whole epistemological construal of knowledge to be mistaken."[1] Paul Ricoeur has attempted "to dig beneath the epistemological enterprise itself, in order to uncover its properly ontological conditions."[2] Jean-Luc Marion has argued that we necessarily misconceive the truth of revelation if we try to conceive it in epistemological terms; he has challenged any attempt to interpret revelation in terms of epistemology. "There are two possible responses: that of validating the *epistemological* interpretation of revelation, or that of challenging it."[3] Epistemology is the study of just *one* way to access truth: knowledge (*episteme*). But there are other ways: mythology is the study of story (*mythos*); axiology is the study of evaluation (*axia*); technology is the study of practical know-how (*techne*).

What kinds of understanding exceed the field of epistemology? And what are the limits of the correspondence theory of truth? What aspects of writing does it obscure? What does it fail to see?

We sense the limits of this view of truth whenever we read writing that is exceptionally bad. Every sentence in a piece of bad writing may be true, in the sense that it corresponds to reality, yet the writing itself may be shallow, confused, vague, simplistic, and crude. Written texts may be true, and yet consist of nothing but platitudes, clichés, received ideas, tautologies, and statements of the obvious. Such writing is at the same time impeccably correct and completely unilluminating. We cannot think clearly about bad writing if we limit our view of truth to the correspondence of thought with reality.

But we sometimes use "truth" to mean something else. Think of the phrase, "the moment of truth." The phrase makes sense to us, but this sense is not completely clear. What does *truth* mean here?

We use this phrase—"the moment of truth"—when something hidden is revealed. If a mother does not know the sex of her unborn child, when she goes into labor we might say that the moment of truth has come. When voters go to the polls in an uncertain election, counting the ballots is the moment of truth. When an experiment can definitively verify or falsify a hypothesis, the moment of truth comes when the results come in. In each case, a moment of truth occurs when what was hidden is revealed. In a moment, we are able to see what has been unseen. Sometimes we can see what was impossible to see before; other times we are all at once able to see something that has escaped our notice even when it was staring us in the face. Truth in this sense is not a matter of correspondence but of revelation, disclosure, manifestation, unconcealment, "illumination."

This view of truth runs through the Western traditions like an underground stream. Thinkers have testified to this experience of truth even if they have not fully articulated it in precise and definite concepts. Augustine wrote that "the truth of a thing is what reveals its essence."[4] Aquinas wrote that "the true is that which manifests and proclaims existences."[5] Joyce followed Aquinas in describing epiphanies as "the revelation of the whatness of a thing."[6] David Tracy wrote: "Conversation accords primacy to one largely forgotten notion of truth: truth as manifestation. Truth manifests itself, and we recognize its rightness . . . . Truth, in its primordial sense, is manifestation."[7] Heidegger argued that this sense of truth as illumination was implicit in the Greek word for truth—*aletheia*—which literally means "un-oblivion" or "un-forgetting": "The Greek word for truth—one can hardly remind oneself of this too often—is ἀλήθεια [*aletheia*], *unhiddenness*. Something true is ἀληθές [*alethes*], unhidden."[8] Heidegger did not aim to give a new sense to the word "truth"; he aimed to explicate, clarify, and refine an understanding of truth implicit in the philosophical traditions of the West.

How can writing be true in this sense?

At its best, writing does not just refer to things that are already seen and known; instead, it points to what has so far escaped our notice and so illuminates what we have failed to see even when it was right in front of us.

Homer described this illumination in *The Odyssey*. When Penelope wove a shroud by day and secretly unraveled it at night, unbeknownst to the suitors, Homer says: "For three years by her wiles she went unnoticed by and beguiled the Achaians"[9] The phrase "went unnoticed" translates the word *elethe* (ἔληθε), which here means to be concealed by oblivion or *lethe* (λήθη), to go unnoticed, to hide in plain sight. The suitors are living in untruth, in the darkness of oblivion, because they cannot see what is staring them in the face. It is only when a slave girl speaks up that the suitors are able to see what is going on. The words of the slave girl uncover and illuminate what had been hiding in plain sight. The Greek word for truth (*aletheia*) is the opposite of the word for the blindness (*lethe*) that afflicts the suitors. *Aletheia* literally means "un-oblivion" or "unforgetting," and it points to this experience of uncovering and illumination. The slave girl's words are true not just because they correspond to reality, but because they uncover what had been hidden. In the deepest sense, words are true when they illuminate something and let it be seen for what it is.

Homer describes this experience in another passage as well: When Odysseus finally returns to Ithaca, after being away for twenty years, he cannot see his homeland for what it is. His eyes register the landscape, but he does not recognize it as the place he grew up. Homer says: "But Odysseus awoke out of his sleep in his native land, and did not recognize it, having been away so long. For about him the goddess had shed a mist, Pallas Athena, daughter of Zeus . . . Therefore, all things seemed strange to their ruler."[10] Odysseus cannot see Ithaca for what it is until Athena points it out to him in words: "'I will show you the land of Ithaca' . . . . So spoke the goddess, and scattered the mist, and the land appeared."[11] Note the link between *speaking*, *scattering the mist*, and *letting Ithaca appear* as such. The identity of his homeland is hiding in plain sight until it is revealed or unconcealed by words. Athena's words are true not just in the sense that they correspond to the world, but in the sense that they scatter the mist of *lethe* and let the world appear as it is.

Proust described this illumination in *Swann's Way* when he wrote about the experience of reading his favorite author.

> Whenever he spoke of something whose beauty had until then remained hidden [*jusque-là cachée*] from me, of pine forests or of hailstorms, of Notre-Dame Cathedral, of Athalie or of Phèdre, by some image he would make their beauty explode into my consciousness. And so, realizing how many parts of the universe there were that my feeble perception would be powerless to discern if he did not bring them within my reach, I longed to have some opinion, some metaphor of his, about everything in the world, and especially about the things that I might someday have the opportunity to see for myself.[12]

Proust is describing the revelatory power of words. Words may point out what we habitually overlook—what remains invisible to us even as it stares us in the face—and so reveal what was hidden by our obliviousness. Literature does not just transport us into a fictive world; it gives us words that reveal more clearly the world in which we actually live. At its best, the experience of reading is an experience of revelation.

This kind of revelation also comes in the practice of writing. Rilke said that authentic writing starts with a movement away from the superficial clarity of everyday discourse toward something we have obscurely felt, something that exceeds our grasp and for which we have no words. To write is to follow that feeling and reach beyond the limits of our comprehension, to fumble in the darkness for words that can grasp what has been obscure and bring it into the light of understanding.

> To let each impression and each embryo of a feeling come to completion, entirely in itself, in the dark, in the unsayable [*im Dunkel, im Unsagbaren*], the unconscious, beyond the reach of one's own understanding [*dem eigenen Verstande Unerreichbaren*], and with deep humility and patience to wait for the hour when a new clarity [*einer neuen Klarheit*] is born: this alone is what it means to live as an artist: in understanding as in creating.[13]

Writing for Rilke is a struggle not just to reflect what is already seen, but to illuminate what is obscure. At its best, writing aims not just at truth as correspondence, but at truth as illumination.

The locus of truth in this sense is not the proposition. Propositions may be true, but the world may also be illuminated by images, metaphors, descriptions, questions, and stories.

On a deeper level, the truth of writing in this sense is not just a matter of content but also of style. Styles of writing articulate ways of thinking and feeling. A text whose style conveys a new way of thought and feeling may allow us to see the world in a new light. Writing illuminates human existence not just through its paraphrasable content but through its style. The link between style and vision was clearly laid out by Proust:

> Style for the writer, no less than color for the painter, is a question not of technique but of vision: it is the revelation [*révélation*], which by direct and conscious methods would be impossible, of the qualitative difference, the uniqueness of the fashion in which the world appears to each one of us, a difference which, if there were no art, would remain forever the secret of every individual.[14]

We convey our understanding of things not just through *what* we write, but also unconsciously through our *way* of writing. The question of style is bound to the question of understanding.

Writing at its best aims at truth. True writing is good, while bad writing is somehow untrue: mistaken, mendacious, delusional, deceitful, empty, idle, inauthentic, or bullshit. But what is the link between truth and goodness—between the veridical and the ethical dimensions of writing? In what sense does writing have an ethical dimension? What is ethics? How is ethics linked to the search for truth? How are questions of ethics related to the question of how to write?

GOODNESS

What makes writing good? This question is commonly answered in four ways:

1. Writing is good when it gives *pleasure*. It is bad when it is ugly, awkward, witless, and dull. The reason most academic prose is bad, in this view, is that it is written by academics, that is, by people who are used to having a captive audience. Lecturers tend not to become great writers for the same reason that prison cooks tend not to become great chefs. Academic writing is also supposed to be serious, and most people can't tell the difference between seriousness and witlessness. As Nietzsche wrote: "For most people, the intellect is an awkward, gloomy, creaking machine that is hard to start; when they want to work with this machine and think well, they call it 'taking the matter *seriously*.'"[1] Nietzsche is right: the mark of true seriousness is not awkward, gloomy, laborious prose, but an unconditional commitment to truth, and that commitment is perfectly compatible with grace, elegance, wit, and beauty. So there is some truth to the view that writing is good when it gives pleasure, and bad

when it is painful to read (the *hedonic* view of writing). But it is also true that writing is bad when it aims *only* at pleasure, for example, mindless entertainment, meaningless beauty, cheap laughs. The greatest pleasure comes from writing that aims at something higher than pleasure: wit that reveals the gap between polite fictions and reality; eloquence that distills insights to their essence; inventions that stretch the bounds of the sayable; beauty that calls us back to what matters. The most serious writing shines with the virtues essential to the search for truth, and it is just this writing that gives the highest pleasure. Good writing gives pleasure, but pleasure alone is not the measure of good writing.

2. Writing is good when it is *well-crafted*. Quality comes from craft, and craft is a matter of technique. This is the *technical* view of writing, and to some extent it is true: writing is rarely any good without the long, hard discipline of craftsmanship. But craftsmanship is not enough. The quality of a craftsman's work is measured by the quality of the work done by the crafted product itself. No matter how beautifully finished a piano may be, it is not well-crafted if it doesn't actually work. So technical excellence cannot be the sole measure of good writing. Technique is only a means to an end; what matters is how well writing serves its purpose.

3. Writing is good when it *works*. As a means to an end, writing is good insofar as it effects the end it is meant to serve. Good means effective. This is the *instrumental* view of writing—writing has no intrinsic purpose; it is good or bad only in relation to the purpose for which it is used. But effectiveness is never an end in itself— we also judge writing by the ends it aims to effect. We usually don't speak of "effective" hate speech, "excellent" propaganda, or "outstanding" sophistry. We hesitate to say writing is good even if, in purely instrumental terms, it is a masterpiece of plagiarism and bullshit. We judge writing not just by how well it works, but also by what it does.

4. Writing is good when it is *moral*. Since all writing aims at some end, we can judge writing by the ends it serves. And these ends are never merely technical or instrumental, but always moral or immoral as well. No matter how well-crafted and effective it is, we tend not to say that writing is good if it is hateful, mendacious, manipulative, malevolent, violent, or false. We judge writing by whether it is truthful and just. It is myopic to separate good writing from moral goodness. Writing is good, in this view, when the ends it serves are moral.

These four answers are not wrong, but the concepts they take for granted seem limited. We sense these limits, again, when we read writing that is exceptionally bad—writing whose badness exceeds the standards by which we usually evaluate written texts.

Think of the words we use for good writing. We don't just say it is moral, effective, well-crafted, and true. Nor merely that it is deep, clear, precise, complex, and refined. We also say it is disciplined, thoughtful, lucid, brilliant, generous, charitable, witty, or wise.

Same with words for bad writing: we don't just say bad writing is untrue, incompetent, ineffective, or immoral. Nor do we stop at saying it is shallow, confused, vague, simplistic, and crude. Bad writing can also be lazy, undisciplined, witless, glib, pedantic, boorish, buffoonish, facile, vacuous, pretentious, bombastic, pompous, smug, self-indulgent, obsequious, craven, ungenerous, polemical, violent, myopic, mediocre, and profoundly stupid.

These words are not *hedonic*. They are not *technical*. They are not *instrumental*. They are not even *moral*, in the strict sense of the word. (Stupidity is not immoral, except when it is deliberate.)

These words are *ethical*. They concern one's *ethos* or character. Character is commonly understood as the part of the soul that feels and desires—the non-rational part of the soul that may be trained to listen to reason.[2] But the Greek word *ethos* (ἦθος) points to something broader and deeper than common notions of character: it points to the understanding of how to live that governs our usual ways of being in the world, being with others, and being toward ourselves.

Every ethos is oriented by a vision of the good in the highest sense. This sense of goodness was denoted by the ancient Greek word *agathos* (ἀγαθός). The word primarily applies not to actions but to ways of being that are felt to be worthy of honor and intrinsically worthwhile. *Agathos* names not what it is right to do, but what it is good to be.

An *ethos* in this sense is rooted in the basic traits of human existence: our *vision* of the good; our *understanding* of beings; the habitual *feelings* through which we sense what matters; the *languages* in which we think; the *practices* through which we pursue various goods; the *ideals* we live for; the *virtues* that let us approach these ideals; the *heroes* who embody these virtues; the *stories* of how they lived; the *values* that govern what we care about; the *temperament* conducive to a good life; the *mores* that guide our relations to others, and the *formative experiences* in whose light we see the possibilities of human life. These traits make up our character. We do not just *have* an ethos; we *are* an ethos.

A number of philosophers have argued that ethical thought in this sense is broader and deeper than moral reasoning. Paul Ricoeur argued that morality presupposes an understanding of the good that is properly called ethical: "ethics has primacy over morality."[3] Charles Taylor argued that moral philosophy has narrowed our thinking about the good life: "the 'moral' encompasses a domain significantly narrower than what ancient philosophers defined as the 'ethical.'"[4] Bernard Williams argued that, "morality should be understood as a particular development of the ethical."[5] The point here is not to junk, trash, or discard morality. The point is to circumscribe the limits of moral thought. I have nothing against morality—some of my best friends are moral. But we have to ask about the limits within which moral thought makes sense, and beyond which it is bound to distort or blind our vision of the good. What kinds of good writing exceed moral concepts of goodness? How does this notion of ethics help us understand in what ways writing can be good? In what sense does writing have an ethical dimension?

Our ethos governs the ways we relate to the world, to others, and to ourselves. These relations structure the act of writing: we write *about* things, in response *to* others, *for* an audience, and *for* ourselves. Writing has an ethical dimension in the sense that how we write is rooted in who we are. Questions of how to write are ultimately rooted in questions of how to live.

Four questions stand out.

What are the ethics of *writing about things*? Of good writing we say "it does justice" to its topic. It is fair. It looks at all sides. It respects the distinctive nature of the topic and tries to show it for what it is. Of bad writing, we say "it does violence" to its topic. It distorts the topic, deforms its nature, mangles its order, obliterates essential distinctions, and forces it into a Procrustean framework of thoughtless preconceptions.

Words can do violence to things in several ways. One kind of violence is done by language that is *shallow*—language that points to a single obvious side of things while obscuring what is less obvious but more essential. Another violence is done by language that is *confused*—that effaces distinctions between words or blurs essential differences. There is also the violence of *vague* language, which descends on things like a cloud of acid that corrodes their contours and reduces them to undifferentiated matter. There is the violence of *simplistic* writing, which forces complex realities into facile and familiar schemas. And then there is the violence of writing whose terms are too *crude* to incisively distinguish things and grasp precisely what they are, like someone trying to do brain surgery with a hacksaw and a rusty pair of pliers.

What are the ethics of *writing on others*? Again it is a matter of justice and violence. But there are different levels of violence toward others in writing. On the most obvious level, there is verbal abuse: hate speech, invective, dehumanization, demonization, insults, profanity, slurs, stereotypes, clichés, tokenism, and idealization. On a deeper level, there are polemics—writing that turns words into weapons and approaches others as enemies to be attacked, demolished, defeated, and destroyed. On the most basic level, there is the violence of objectification—writing that approaches others only as objects of knowledge and not as possible sources of insight. This violence is implicit in writing that speaks *about* others but not *with* them, that aims to learn *about* others but not *from* them. This kind of writing categorizes, classifies, analyzes, diagnoses, and explains, but fails to listen, to learn the language of others, and to be open to other points of view. It relates to the other as an "it" instead of a "you"—it adopts a stance of mastery instead of dialogue.

What are the ethics of *writing for others*? The highest aim of writing, in relation to others, is not to defeat them through sophistry, or have our way through manipulation, or to impress them with shows of erudition, or to put on displays of technical virtuosity, or to vent emotions, or to express inchoate thoughts. Insofar as we write *for* others, the highest aim of writing is to *communicate*. In one sense, to communicate is to see something, to put it into words, and thereby to make it visible to others. In another sense, it is to write in a way that conveys to others an emotional attunement to the world. In a third sense, to communicate is to feel the impact of reality, to capture it in language, and to convey the force of that impact to others. Communication is not just a matter of transmitting ideas or feelings from one mind to another. Heidegger made this point in *Being and Time*: "Communication is never anything like a conveying of experiences, for example, opinions and wishes, from the inside of one subject to the inside of another."[6] Instead, communication is a matter of leading others to the point where they can share our standpoint, a standpoint to which beings show themselves to some extent for what they are. Even more, to communicate is to open others to the world and put them in touch with reality, so that the force of that touch is felt in the depths of their being. This requires more than sincerity and good intentions. It requires the long, hard, patient labor of gathering one's thoughts and laying them out in a coherent sequence of steps. And it requires moving people with words, conveying enough passion to move them from their usual place in the world. Writing is building a path of thought in which each step follows from the previous step and leads to the next, and at the end of which readers see the world from a new point of view.

For whom should one write? The greatest thinkers do not write in the esoteric language of a tiny elite, nor in commonplaces that are immediately clear to everyone. Instead, they start with the most common and accessible words and refine them to the point where they can articulate the highest levels of thought. But in the end, they do not just write for others; they write for themselves.

What are the ethics of writing for oneself?

Writing for oneself has a bad reputation, and this reputation is mostly well-deserved. Such writing tends to be self-indulgent scribbling. In response to this kind of scribbling, many teachers advise students *not* to write for themselves: the novice's "natural tendency as a writer is to think primarily of himself—hence to write primarily for himself. Here, in a nutshell, lies the ultimate reason for most bad writing."[7] The way to write well, in this all-too-common view, is not to write for oneself, but to model writing on conversation.

Here again we should listen to actual writers more than specialists in composition. T. S. Eliot wrote that, "my advice to 'up and coming writers' is, don't write at first for anyone but yourself."[8] Rachel Carson said, "If you write what you yourself sincerely think and feel and are interested in, the chances are very high that you will interest other people as well."[9] Rilke told a young poet not to think of how his work would be received, but to turn inward and, "as if no one had ever tried before, try to say what you see and feel and love and lose"—"And if out of this turning-within, out of this immersion in your own world, *poems* come, then you will not think of asking anyone if they are good or not."[10] The best writing is not primarily aimed at an audience but at truth. People want to hear a voice that is singular, incisive, authentic, illuminating—a voice that moves them from their usual standpoint and leads them beyond familiar horizons of thought. In the words of Maurice Blanchot: "This is why it is dangerous to write for other people, in order to evoke the speech of others and reveal them to themselves: the fact is that other people do not want to hear their own voices; they want to hear someone else's voice, a voice that is real, profound, troubling like the truth."[11]

This kind of voice comes from another way of writing for oneself. For some thinkers—Epictetus, Nietzsche, Arendt, Foucault, Anzaldúa, Morrison—writing is a path to understanding. Not a tool to communicate what we already have in mind, but a practice through which we can deepen, clarify, and refine our own way of thinking.

The model for this kind of writing is not conversation but *meditation*—the solitary inner speech through which we come back to ourselves and do the work of forming and transforming how we think. Proust wrote that his first attempts at writing were mediocre precisely because they were modeled on conversation:

> Though conducted in silence, this exercise was nonetheless a conversation and not a meditation [*cet exercice était pourtant une conversation et non une méditation*], my solitude a mental social round in which it was not I myself but imaginary interlocutors who controlled my choice of words, and . . . I formulated, instead of the thoughts that I believed to be true, those that came easily to my mind.[12]

In order to move toward truth, he suggested, we have to model writing not on conversation but on solitary meditation.

> When we have arrived at reality, we must, to express it and preserve it, prevent the intrusion of all those extraneous elements which at every moment the gathered speed of habit lays at our feet. Above all, we should have to be on guard against those phrases which are chosen rather by the lips than by the mind, those humorous phrases such as we utter in conversation and continue, at the end of a long conversation with other people, to address factitiously to ourselves, although they merely fill our mind with lies . . . real books should be the offspring not of daylight and casual talk, but of darkness and silence.[13]

Proust's book itself is an instance of writing as meditation. In reading his novel, we sense we are following the path of a thinker whose highest concern was the search for truth, and for whom writing was the movement of straying beyond the limits of everyday discourse, and the long, slow, laborious, and inspired work of inventing a discourse able to grasp and bring to light the truth of experiences long hidden in darkness and silence.

Meditation is a form of thought that aims to form our ethos in order to enable us to live in the truth. This is the deepest sense in which writing has an ethical dimension—it is a practice through which we form, reform, and transform who we are.

Still, this conclusion seems incomplete. Yes, writing may have an ethical dimension. But good writing is also beautiful. Beauty is the most obvious trait that makes writing good. What then is the relation of beauty and goodness? How are they related to truth? Today, questions of beauty, goodness, and truth are commonly supposed to be separate and distinct. But perhaps the beauty of writing eludes common concepts of beauty and pushes us to rethink the nature of beauty itself.

BEAUTY

Beauty is commonly viewed in several ways.

One view sees beauty as the sensible appearance of the ideal. Plotinus wrote that, "We hold that all loveliness of this world comes by communion in Ideal-Form."[1] Hegel wrote that, "the beautiful is characterized as the pure appearance of the Idea to sense."[2] In this conception, things are beautiful insofar as they manifest their ideal form. Think of circles. Perfect circles are beautiful, in this view, because they manifest the ideal form of a circle. In the same way, human bodies are beautiful to the extent that they more or less perfectly embody the ideal form of a human being. Philosophers call this an "ontological" concept of beauty since it links beauty to what things are in essence.

Another conception of beauty belongs to the field of aesthetics. The word "aesthetics" was coined by Alexander Baumgarten in 1735 to name a sphere of thought separate from knowledge or morality. Baumgarten argued that beauty does not belong to the sphere of knowledge, since it is not an objective trait of beings that can be known through logic, theory, and empirical science. Nor does beauty belong to the sphere of morality, since it is perceived by irrational feelings rather than by the rational faculties through which we grasp what is morally right. Beauty cannot be grasped by reason, but only felt by the sub-rational faculties of sensation, imagination, fancy, wit, and taste. Since these faculties perceive beauty through feeling, Baumgarten named their proper sphere with the Greek word for "feeling"—*aesthetics*.[3]

Aesthetic thinkers have distinguished two kinds of beauty.[4]

Beauty is "*dependent*" when it depends on our ideas. Our ideas of beings include a concept of their purpose or end. When beings fulfill their end, we see them as perfect, and when this perfection appears to the senses, we find them beautiful. Things are beautiful, in this sense, when they conform to our ideas of what they are and ought to be. So beauty depends on our ideas, and these ideas may be arbitrary. One culture may find tan skin common and pale skin beautiful since the first evokes rustic drudgery and the second evokes a sheltered life of luxury and refinement. Another culture may find tan skin beautiful and pale skin common since the former signifies a life of athletic leisure, while the latter indicates a life of wage slavery under fluorescent lights. Neither pale nor tan skin is beautiful in themselves, in this view. And what is true of skin color is true of everything. Nothing is beautiful in itself. Beauty is no longer in beings, but in the eye of the beholder.

Beauty is *"free"* when it is independent of our ideas. We sometimes find things beautiful even when we have no idea what they are or what they are for, and we take pleasure in their order, pattern, harmony, color, and proportion apart from any concept of their nature or purpose. We tend to find flowers beautiful, for example, whether or not we have any idea of what they are for. The same is true of the logarithmic spirals of seashells. We also find beauty in non-representational art, in the pure play of forms, or the pure presence of matter, apart from any link to goodness or truth.

The beauty of writing can be understood in these terms *to some extent*. Writing is beautiful, in an ontological sense, when it represents beings in their ideal form, or when it approaches the ideal of perfect communication. Writing has a kind of dependent beauty when it represents our ideas of what things are, or when it itself embodies our idea of what writing is and ought to be. And writing is also beautiful, in the sense of free beauty, when it manifests the pure beauty of form, pattern, sound, tone, symmetry, complexity, tension, harmony, and order.

These different views have generated much debate. Some claim that the formal beauty of aesthetic objects transcends culture and time because it harmonizes with the universal faculties of human feeling.[5] Others argue that we cannot understand beauty if we do not see it as belonging to the form of beings themselves.[6] Still others argue that our sense of beauty depends on cultural ideals, and these ideals are always implicated in relations of power: "No judgment of taste is innocent."[7] Despite the differences between them, all of these views are now thought to belong to the field of aesthetics.

But a number of philosophers have called into question aesthetic approaches to beauty and art. Heidegger argued that aesthetics obscures the nature of art: "For aesthetics, art is the display of the beautiful in the sense of the pleasant, the agreeable. And yet art is the opening up of the Being of beings."[8] Hans-Georg Gadamer argued that art cannot be fully understood in terms of aesthetics: "My thesis, then, is that the being of art cannot be defined as an object of an aesthetic consciousness."[9] Giorgio Agamben aimed "to purify the concept of 'beauty' by filtering out the αἴσθησις [*aesthesis*]." In his view, "Perhaps nothing is more urgent—if we really want to engage the problem of art in our time, than a *destruction* of aesthetics that would, by clearing away what is usually taken for granted, allow us to bring into question the very meaning of aesthetics as the science of the work of art."[10] And Karsten Harries aimed "to call into question the aesthetic approach that had for so long presided over the progress of art."[11] What then are the limits of aesthetic approaches to art and beauty? What do they fail to see?

Aesthetic thought obscures another kind of beauty. An understanding of this beauty is implicit in the ancient Greek word *kalos* (καλός), which has no strict equivalent in modern English. *Kalos* can be translated as *beautiful*, but also as *handsome, lovely, fine, genuine, noble, virtuous, honorable*, and *good*. The opposite of *kalos* is *aischros* (αἰσχρός), which can mean *ugly*, but also *shameful, base, ignoble, vicious, disgraceful, dishonorable,* and *bad*.

Something is beautiful, in the sense of *kalos*, when it shows the virtues essential to a good life. There is an intrinsic link between this kind of beauty and virtue. Aristotle laid out this view of beauty in the *Eudemian Ethics*: "What are beautiful [*kalos*] are the virtues, and the actions that come from virtue."[12] An action is beautiful, in this sense, when it exemplifies a virtue without which it is not possible to live well: both the virtues of character, such as courage, temperance, and justice; and the intellectual virtues: know-how, discernment, deliberation, judgment, intellect, knowledge, and wisdom.[13]

Beauty in this sense is intrinsically linked to goodness. Plato emphasized this link when he wrote, "I say that the good is beautiful [*kalos*]."[14] Marcus Aurelius made this connection when he wrote that he had "understood the nature of the good, that it is beautiful [*kalos*], and the nature of the bad, that is it ugly [*aischros*]."[15] Nietzsche also took this link for granted when he wrote that beauty is the sensible appearance of what we experience as the highest good: "In *my* view what is beautiful (observed historically) is what is visible in the most honored men of an era, as an expression of what is *most worthy* of honor."[16] In this sense, beauty is the shining appearance of the highest goods.

How can writing be beautiful in this sense? What does it mean for writing to be *kalos*?

In one sense, writing is beautiful when it *portrays* an action that shows real virtue. Action is beautiful when virtue shines through it, and writing is beautiful when it limns the beauty of action. Think of *The Iliad*. The final showdown between Hector and Achilles is strangely beautiful, to us as well as to Homer, because it is *kalos* (beautiful) to walk out into danger to protect others, and *aischros* (ugly) to shrink back and let others fight in one's place.[17] The beauty of the portrayal comes from the beauty of the action portrayed, and the action is beautiful because it manifests so clearly the nature of courage. The same kind of beauty appears in a very different context (Jn 10:11) where a good shepherd is said to be *kalos*: "I am the good [*kalos*] shepherd. The good [*kalos*] shepherd lays down his life for his sheep."[18] The shepherd is beautiful because his actions embody pure love, and his story is beautiful because it portrays those actions. Writing is beautiful, in this sense, when it depicts moments in which the highest virtues are manifested in action and speech.

In another sense, writing is beautiful when its *style* of portrayal harmonizes with the topic portrayed. When Thoreau described his life by Walden Pond, for example, the simplicity of his style evoked the ideal of a life raised to the bare essentials.

> I went to the woods because I wished to live deliberately, to front only the essential facts of life, and see if I could not learn what it had to teach, and not, when I came to die, discover than I had not lived.[19]

Thoreau moved to the woods to simplify his life, to remove the distractions that divert us from what really matters, and the virtue of simplicity is embodied in the spareness of his writing, which shuns any clutter that might obscure his basic point. His motto, "Simplify, simplify" applies not just to his art of living but to his art of writing. His style is beautiful because it manifests the virtue it describes.

But writing can also be beautiful when a way of speaking *itself*, apart from its subject matter, manifests the virtues of character, intellect, and spirit. We find writing beautiful in this way when the sheer brilliance of a writer shines through her words. The beauty of writing in this sense does not come from *what* is portrayed but from the *style* of portrayal.

This beauty appears most clearly where there is the greatest contrast between the brilliance of a style and the ugliness of the subject. Just as the splendor of a background is most highlighted when the object in the foreground is ultra-black, so the beauty of style is clearest when the subject matter is especially vile and disgraceful.

What then is an example of purely stylistic beauty? In what text does the writing manifest the highest virtues even as it portrays the basest and nastiest vices?

Take Max Scheler on *ressentiment*. His writing is beautiful because it is a miracle of empathy and intelligence, even when he is writing about the lowest and darkest depths of the soul:

> To its very core, the mind of *ressentiment* man is filled with envy, the impulse to detract, malice, and secret vindictiveness. These affects have become fixed attitudes, detached from all determinate objects. Independently of his will, this man's attention will be instinctively drawn by all events which can set these affects in motion . . . [*Ressentiment* man] has the urge to scold, to depreciate, to belittle whatever he can.[20]

Has anyone described blindness with greater insight? Scheler is perhaps outdone only by Nietzsche himself when he lays out the logic underlying the impulse to punish: "To watch someone suffer is nice; to make someone suffer is even nicer."[21] The odd beauty of this sentence comes from the blunt juxtaposition of style and subject—the naked ugliness of the sentiment described and the brilliant wit of the description. Writing tends to be beautiful, no matter what it is about, when its style manifests the virtues—patience, care, thoughtfulness, judgment, empathy, courage, tenacity, and wit—required to see what has gone unnoticed and to make it visible by putting it into words.

This kind of beauty is the key to a seeming paradox: Nothing is more dispiriting than a beautiful subject depicted in a crude, witless, and myopic way, so that the ugliness of the portrayal contaminates and overpowers the beauty of what is portrayed. This is why "heartwarming" stories, if they are sufficiently stupid, make one want to blow one's brains out. But it is also why we can be healed and inspired by writing that portrays even the ugliest realities of human life, as long as that ugliness is portrayed in a kind, thoughtful, just, and brilliantly intelligent way. Writing at its best does not beautify ugliness or aestheticize the darkest recesses of the human soul, but faces the darkness and illuminates it with words that shine with honesty, courage, justice, and wisdom.

Beauty in this sense is intrinsically linked to truth and goodness. This link is clear in Plato's remarks on writing that is beautiful in the sense of *kalos*. In the *Phaedrus*, he asks bluntly, "What then is the way to write beautifully [*kalos*] or not?" More precisely: "If speech is to be beautiful [*kalos*], must not the mind of the speaker know the truth of the matter on which he is to speak?"[22] This question is absurd if we understand beauty in aesthetic terms—writing can of course be untrue and aesthetically beautiful at the same time. But if we understand beauty as the appearance of the virtues, then Plato's question makes sense. Writing is ugly in the sense of *aischros* (worthless and disgraceful) when it reveals that the speaker is too thoughtless, craven, or mendacious to say what is true; it is beautiful in the sense of *kalos* when it shines with the honesty, courage, intelligence, and thoughtfulness essential to the search for truth. This is why, for Plato, speech cannot be beautiful (*kalos*) if it is not true (*alethes*). "As the Spartans say, there is not and never will be a real art of speaking which does not say the truth [*aletheia*]."[23]

So beautiful writing may be illuminating in two ways. It can shed light on a subject by making clear what had been unnoticed or obscure. In this sense, we say that writing is "brilliant" when it lets us see something we could not see on our own. But writing is also illuminating when the virtues proper to the search for truth shine through its style, as when we speak of "radiant intelligence" or "scintillating wit." The shining appearance of the highest virtues is a kind of beauty, and writing that is beautiful in this sense can itself illuminate the highest possibilities of human existence.

Writing is beautiful when it is luminous.

INSPIRATION

In the *Phaedrus*, Plato wrote that writing is a craft [*techne*], but that craftsmanship alone is not enough to compose great writing. To write at the highest level, Socrates argues, we need not just craft but inspiration.

> From the Muses comes a kind of possession and madness [*mania*], which takes hold of a gentle and pure soul, arousing and inspiring it to songs and other poetry.... Whoever comes to the doors of poetry without the madness of the Muses, convinced that he will be a good poet by skill [*techne*] alone, will fall short, and his poetry will be nothing next to the poetry of the inspired madman.[1]

Plato's words are worth unpacking with some care. Inspiration is said to be a kind of madness or mania that alters our state of mind, but this alteration is said to be akin to waking up. The word translated as "arousing" (ἐγείρουσα) means rousing us from sleep, opening our eyes, bringing us back to ourselves, shaking us in a way that removes us from oblivion and lets us see the world as it is. The word translated as "inspiring" (ἐκβακχεύουσα) literally means being overcome by Bacchus (Dionysus). To be inspired in this sense is to be under the influence of something that changes how we see, to be infused with a power that is not our own, to be filled with passion, to be *enthused* in the original sense of being entered into (*en-*) by a god (*theos*). The experience of inspiration is the experience of being touched and shaken awake, so that we see what we could not see before, and so that this new sight impassions and empowers us to write what we could not write through effort and craft alone.[2]

Many other writers have testified to the experience of inspiration. Hesiod wrote that the Muses "breathed a divine voice into me."[3] Homer described poetry as a mix of human craft and divine gift: "I taught myself the craft, but a god has planted deep in my spirit all the paths of song."[4] Shelley described the experience from which his best poetry came: "We are aware of evanescent visitations of thought and feeling sometimes associated with place or person, sometimes regarding our own mind alone, and always arising unforeseen and departing unbidden, but elevating and delightful beyond all expression.... It is as it were the interpenetration of a diviner nature through our own."[5] But inspiration is not confined to poets. It has also been described by writers of philosophy, music, science, and math. The chemist Dmitri Mendeleev, for example, wrote that he first envisioned the periodic table when he was asleep. "I saw in a dream a table where all elements fell into place as required. Awakening, I immediately wrote it down on a piece of paper, only in one place did a correction later seem necessary."[6]

Perhaps the most precise description of inspiration comes from Nietzsche, whose words are worth quoting at length.

> Has anyone today a distinct conception of what poets of strong ages called inspiration? If not, I will describe it.—If one had the slightest residue of superstition left in one, one would hardly be able to set aside the idea that one is merely incarnation, merely mouthpiece, merely medium of overwhelming forces. The concept of revelation, in the sense that something suddenly, with unspeakable certainty and subtlety, becomes visible, audible, something that shakes and overturns one to the depths, simply describes the fact. One hears, one does not seek; one takes, one does not ask who gives; a thought flashes up like lightning, with necessity, unfalteringly formed—I have never had any choice. An ecstasy whose tremendous tension sometimes discharges itself in a flood of tears, while one's steps now involuntarily rush along, now involuntarily lag; a complete being outside oneself. . . . Everything is in the highest degree involuntary, but takes place in a tempest of a feeling of freedom, of unconditionedness, of power, of divinity.[7]

These words deserve to be read with some care. In his description, Nietzsche makes four key points.

First, inspiration is a fact of experience: "The concept of revelation . . . simply describes the fact."[8] We may dismiss all superstition, renounce magical thinking, detach the experience of inspiration from the myths in which it has been understood, and try to translate those myths into precise and rigorous concepts. But we are not entitled to neglect the phenomenon of inspiration simply because we can no longer understand it in mythical terms. Writers throughout the ages have experienced inspiration. The phenomenon of inspiration is simply a matter of fact.

Second, inspiration is an experience of illumination: "Something suddenly, with unspeakable certainty and subtlety, becomes *visible*, audible . . . a thought flashes up like lightning."[9] Lightning is a classic figure for revelation: just as a bolt of lightning may reveal what had been hidden in darkness, so too inspiration may reveal what has been hidden in oblivion. The figure implies that inspiration may be a source of truth, as long as truth is understood not as correctness but as illumination (*aletheia*).

Third, inspiration involves both will and will-lessness—a voluntary doing within an involuntary state of mind: "one hears, one does not seek; one takes, one does not ask who gives."[10] Nietzsche emphasizes the passive, will-less, involuntary nature of the experience: inspiration cannot be summoned at will; the experience of illumination, like the experience of lightning, is beyond foresight and control. But the experience is not wholly passive: one must take what is given, see what is revealed, and give words to what is shown in that revelation. Writing while inspired is not a matter of taking dictation from a higher power, not transcribing a discourse that is already perfect and complete. It is a matter of finding words for what is revealed in a new light: "all existence here wants to become words, all becoming here wants to learn speech from you."[11]

Last, inspiration is an experience of the divine: "Everything is in the highest degree involuntary, but takes place as in a tempest of a feeling of freedom, of unconditionedness, of power, of divinity [*Göttlichkeit*]."[12] These words seem both strange and familiar. They are familiar in that Nietzsche echoes the many thinkers—Homer, Hesiod, Plato, Shelley—who linked inspiration to the divine. They are strange because Nietzsche was writing at a time when most people no longer believed in the existence of the Muses, and because Nietzsche himself is commonly supposed to have been an atheist. How are we to understand this reference to divinity?

Nietzsche's words are strange because they belong to a level of thought that precedes any theism, atheism, or agnosticism. These three positions—theism, atheism, agnosticism—are all answers to a single question: Does God (do gods) exist? Theists answer: Yes. Atheists answer: No. Agnostics answer that they do not know. But any answer to this question must already take for granted some view of who or what a god is. We cannot affirm or deny or suspend judgment on the *existence* of a divinity without first understanding the *meaning* of divinity itself.

Every theism, atheism, and agnosticism must presuppose some interpretation of the essence of the divine. Nietzsche's thought is strange because he does not just affirm or deny the existence of a particular deity; he questions the essence of divinity—what makes God (or gods) divine.

To understand Nietzsche's words, we have to take three steps. Whenever we read a strange text, our first step is to make sense of it by translating it into familiar terms. This first reading—the reduction of the foreign to the familiar—is bound to be a misreading, but this misreading is inevitable. There is no point pretending we can skip this step; it is better to recognize that our first step is bound to be a misstep. The second step is to learn the language of the text—not to read familiar ways of thought into foreign words, but to learn how foreign words articulate another way of thought. We fully learn a foreign language when we make it our own, that is, when we learn to think in its terms.[13] (This is why, to understand the practice of writing, it helps to learn the ancient Greek words for true, good, and beautiful: *alethes, agathos,* and *kalos.*) To think in a foreign language, we not only have to sense the irreducible differences between foreign and familiar words, but also to see how they reveal the world in different ways. The third step is to see our familiar world in light of the foreign way of thought—not only to open our own perspective on another world, but to open another perspective on our own world. In the case of the *Phaedrus,* for example, our task is not only to see into the world of Plato (to understand the text in its own terms), but also to see the world in which we live from Plato's perspective. And this means to understand in what sense, for Plato, the experience of inspiration is an experience of the divine.

Nietzsche calls us to a new task of thought: rather than interpreting inspiration in terms of our preconceptions of the divine, we should rethink the meaning of divinity in light of the experience of inspiration.

But Nietzsche's description of inspiration is still incomplete. He described with great precision the effortlessness of inspired speech, but he left out the years of effort that artists have to endure before inspiration may strike. It is only through years of effort that effortless creation is possible. It is as if Nietzsche described hang gliding by focusing only on the experience of being lifted into the heights by thermals, while leaving out the long, hard climb up a mountain to a point where catching a thermal is even possible.

The best description of this effort comes from Pyotr Tchaikovsky. Tchaikovsky stressed the importance of inspiration for art, but also stressed the importance of work for inspiration. To make something great, we need to be inspired, he wrote, but for inspiration to come, we have to devote ourselves to our work every day. His words are also worth quoting at length:

Do not believe those who try to persuade you that composition is only a cold exercise of the intellect. The only music capable of moving and touching us is that which flows from the depths of a composer's soul when he is stirred by inspiration. There is no doubt that even the greatest musical geniuses have sometimes worked without inspiration. This guest does not always respond to the first invitation. We must always work, and a self-respecting artist must not fold his hands on the pretext that he is not in the mood. If we wait for the mood, without endeavoring to meet it half-way, we easily become indolent and apathetic. We must be patient, and believe that inspiration will come to those who can master their disinclination. A few days ago I told you I was working every day without any real inspiration. Had I given way to my disinclination, undoubtedly I should have drifted into a long period of idleness. But my patience and faith did not fail me, and to-day I felt that inexplicable glow of inspiration of which I told you; thanks to which I know beforehand that whatever I write to-day will have power to make an impression, and to touch the hearts of those who hear it. I hope you will not think I am indulging in self-laudation, if I tell you that I very seldom suffer from this disinclination to work. I believe the reason for this is that I am naturally patient. I have learnt to master myself, and I am glad I have not followed in the steps of some of my Russian colleagues, who have no self-confidence and are so impatient that at the least difficulty they are ready to throw up the sponge. This is why, in spite of great gifts, they accomplish so little, and that in an amateur way.[14]

Note the link between effort and effortlessness. Yes, the greatest works of art come from effortless bursts of inspiration. But the bursts of inspiration come from long years of hard, patient work. The work of art is not just the fruit of inspiration, but also of the fruitless daily slog toward inspiration itself.

While we cannot summon inspiration at will, we can still create the conditions in which it is more likely to come. One condition is solitude—we need space of our own to sink into concentration. Another is free time—not necessarily years of leisure to lie in bed like Marcel Proust, but just a little time each day to leave the surface of life and descend into the depths. A third is conversation—in the best conversations, ideas emerge that come not from any one person but from the conversation itself. A fourth is contact with the greatest works of others—in that contact, we come under the influence of the spirit that inspired their work. (In this sense, a museum is a temple of the Muses—a place we go to be inspired.) Part of the art of writing is the art of creating the conditions in which inspiration is most likely to strike.

The classic blunder is to wait for inspiration before setting to work. This is like waiting at the foot of a mountain for a thermal to lift our hang glider into the sky. It is not going to happen. We need to lug the hang glider at least halfway up the mountain before we even have a chance of catching a thermal; the higher we go, the more likely we are to catch an updraft and soar above the highest peaks. In the same way, we have to work before we even have a chance of being inspired, but the more we work, the more likely we are to be struck by inspiration and empowered to do what we could never do through effort alone. Near the end of his life, Stendhal wrote *The Charterhouse of Parma* in a burst of inspiration that lasted fifty-two days, but he stressed that those days were the fruit of the years of work he had done before. In his autobiography, he lamented the fact that as a young man he wasted years not working while waiting for inspiration to strike.

> Before writing I always waited for the moment of genius. I was only cured of this mania very belatedly. . . . This foolishness proved very damaging to the quantity of my writings. Even in 1806, I was still waiting for the moment of genius before writing. . . . Had I spoken around 1795 of my intention of writing, some man of good sense would have told me: "Write for two hours every day, genius or no." A remark that would have led to my making use of ten years of my life spent fatuously waiting for *genius*.[15]

If the work of art comes from inspiration, inspiration comes from work.

The proper word for this work is *devotion*. To devote ourselves to something is to give ourselves to it, to love it so much that it becomes a center of gravity in our life, a point around which the rest of our life revolves, a focus of care and attention, to which we gladly give hours of our days and years of our lives. To be a devoted father is to give oneself to one's child. To be a devout musician is to be devoted to the Muses. To be a devoted writer is to give oneself to the work of writing.

But what is the good for the sake of which writers devote themselves to writing? One can devote oneself to writing for the sake of money, fame, or honor. Nothing is more common. And one can also devote oneself to writing for the sake of self-expression, vanity, and the pleasures of graphomania. But writing can also be a path toward understanding, and above all a devotion to the highest kind of understanding—wisdom.

WISDOM

We started with an enigma: Some thinkers see writing not as a tool of communication, or a medium of self-expression, or a substitute for speaking, but as a path to understanding. But how is this possible—how can writing lead to understanding? And how, in particular, can the practice of writing be a search for wisdom?

The point of the last six chapters is that this possibility has been obscured by the most common concepts in which writing is now understood.

1. Language is commonly conceived as a tool of communication or as a medium of self-expression, and these common concepts have obscured the interconnection of language and thought.

2. Thought has been conceived in a narrow and impoverished way—on a model of scientific methods and in light of superficial concepts of truth.

3. The nature of truth has been obscured by the concept of truth as correspondence, which fails to grasp the phenomenon of truth as illumination, and so distorts our view of the *veridical* dimension of writing—the power of writing to tell and show truth.

4. The nature of goodness has been oversimplified by philosophies that conceive the good in either hedonic, technical, instrumental, or moral terms, and this oversimplification has weakened our grasp of the *ethical* dimension of writing—the power of writing to articulate and convey an ethos.

5. The nature of beauty has been veiled by aesthetic concepts of beauty, which have covered over the links between goodness and beauty implicit in the classical Greek word *kalos*. This veiling has hidden the *kallistic* dimension of writing—the beauty of writing that discloses (in content or style) the virtues essential to a good life.

6. The nature of inspiration has been eclipsed by preconceptions of the divine, which have obscured the possibility that writing may be practiced as a form of devotion.

These common concepts belong to modern philosophies that sort truth, goodness, and beauty into separate fields: questions of truth are assigned to epistemology; questions of goodness to moral philosophy; questions of beauty to aesthetics.

But some writers aim at a kind of understanding that transcends these separate fields. Think of Plato. In his portraits of Socrates, Plato made implicit claims to truth: this is who Socrates was; this is a true lover of wisdom; this is what it means to be a philosopher. His claim to truth had an ethical intention: the portraits of Socrates convey his ethos and offer an example of a life worth living. And the ethical intent of the portraits is inseparable from their beauty—they are beautiful not just because the figure of Socrates exemplifies certain virtues, but because Plato's writing itself shines with these virtues—intelligence, thoughtfulness, friendship, wit, courage, temperance, and justice. Plato aimed to beautifully portray a true understanding of a good life. In his writing, truth, goodness, and beauty come together.

We do violence to Plato when we try to force his thought into a framework of modern concepts—if we ask about his "epistemology," his "moral philosophy," and his "aesthetics," as if we could isolate his love of the truth from his love of the good and his love of the beautiful. To do justice to Plato, we have to recognize that he aimed at a kind of understanding in which there is an essential intrication of truth, goodness, and beauty, and that this kind of understanding is divine. The old name for it is *wisdom*.

Wisdom eludes the basic concepts of most philosophy today. It cannot be understood in terms of epistemology, since the truth of wisdom is different from the truth of knowledge; it cannot be verified or reduced to propositions, but is instead the illumination of the goods of human life. Nor can wisdom be understood in terms of moral philosophy. It is good to be moral, but there is more to a good life than being morally good. To be wise is a matter not just of moral reasoning, but of the ideals, virtues, heroes, stories, values, feelings, mores, languages, practices, and experiences that make up our ethos; it concerns not just what it is right to *do*, but what it is good to *be*. And the beauty of wisdom exceeds aesthetic beauty, since it is not a matter of sense perception, but of the shining appearance of the highest virtues in word and action.

Wisdom has traditionally been conceived as one virtue among others. Aristotle laid out this view in the *Nicomachean Ethics*, where he defined wisdom as a theoretical understanding of what is highest: "Wisdom is both scientific knowledge and intuition of what is by nature most honorable."[1] Wisdom in this sense may be the highest virtue of the intellect, but it is a virtue separate and distinct from other virtues of the intellect (skill, cleverness, discernment, deliberation, judgment, prudence, political insight, intellect, and knowledge) as well as from the virtues of character (courage, justice, self-control), to say nothing of the virtues of the spirit (humility, generosity, patience, diligence, charity, temperance, and purity of heart).

But this traditional concept impoverishes our understanding of wisdom and fails to do justice to the way we actually use the word *wisdom* in real life. No matter how much a man might know in theory, we hesitate to call him wise if he falls into a ditch while looking at the stars.[2] Wisdom means something wider and deeper.

The ancient Greek word for wisdom—*sophia*—meant more than knowledge of the highest things. It also meant practical skill, craft, cleverness, cunning, shrewdness, judgment, learning, and prudence.[3] This multiplicity of senses may at first seem perplexing, but if we see how these senses fit together, the coherence of their meanings comes into focus. *Sophia* is not just a vague word that in different contexts happens to mean different things. Instead, *sophia* names the *integration* of all the virtues—the mutual illumination of the virtues proper to practice, theory, character, and spirit. Wisdom is not just one virtue among others; it is the harmony of all the virtues essential to a good life.

But how can we move toward wisdom through the practice of writing? What kind of writing is a path to wisdom?

WRITING AS MEDITATION

Let's go back to one of the quotations from which we started. Michel Foucault said:

> The books I write constitute an experience for me that I'd like to be as rich as possible. An experience is something you come out of changed. If I had to write a book to communicate what I have already thought, I'd never have the courage to begin it. I write because I don't yet know what to think about a subject that attracts my interest. In doing so, the book transforms me, changes what I think. As a consequence, each new work profoundly changes the terms of thinking which I had reached with the previous work. . . . When I write, I do it above all to change myself and not to think the same thing as before.[1]

This experience of writing framed Foucault's view of philosophy. Near the end of his life, he aimed to retrieve and refine the ancient practice of philosophy as a way of life, which was grounded in and guided by a number of assumptions:

Philosophy was a search for wisdom. Pythagoras seems to have been the first to call himself not a wise man but a philosopher—a lover of wisdom—on the grounds that only the gods are wise.[2]

Socrates likewise said he was not a wise man but a lover of wisdom precisely because he knew that he knew nothing noble and good.[3] Augustine also emphasized the search itself: "it is not the discovery but the mere search for wisdom which should be preferred even to the discovery of treasures and to ruling over nations."[4] Later thinkers agreed that to be a philosopher was not to possess wisdom but to search for it. Hugh of St. Victor said simply, "Philosophy is the pursuit of wisdom."[5]

The search for wisdom required a care for the self. Just as athletics and medicine are ways to care for the body, philosophy was a care for the soul. This care for the soul could be called "spiritual," Foucault wrote, if we understand spirituality as the work we do on ourselves in order to move toward truth: "We could call 'spirituality' the search, practices, and experience through which the subject carries out the necessary transformations on himself in order to have access to the truth."[6] Philosophy was a care for the self because it was a search for truth.

The care for the self focused on spiritual exercises. The word for "exercise" in Greek is *askesis*, the root of the English word "ascetic." The notion of philosophy as *askesis* was common in antiquity. Plotinus wrote that: "the soul must be trained."[7] Musonius Rufus wrote that "philosophy is training in nobility of character [*kalokagathias*] and nothing else."[8] Aristotle ridiculed philosophers who took refuge in arguments and did not actually *do* the practices that would transform their souls:

"they are like invalids who listen carefully to their doctors, but who do not do what they are told. Just as such treatment will not make the invalids healthy in body, so this kind of philosophy will not make people healthy in soul."[9] Ancient philosophy included the practice of "ascetics," Foucault argued, in the sense that philosophy was a training of the soul. "Ascetics . . . [is] the more or less coordinated set of exercises that are available, recommended, and even obligatory, and anyway utilizable by individuals in a moral, philosophical, and religious system in order to achieve a definite spiritual objective."[10]

Spiritual exercises aimed to form, reform, and transform one's ethos. To describe this transformation, Foucault retrieved the Greek word *ethopoiesis*, which named the kind of practices that change our character. "The Greeks had a very interesting word, which can be found in Plutarch as well as in Dionysius of Halicarnassus . . . . *Ethopoiein* means making *ethos*, producing *ethos*, changing, transforming *ethos*, the individual's way of being, his mode of existence. *Ethopoios* is something that possesses the quality of transforming an individual's mode of being."[11] The aim of philosophical exercises, in this view, was not just to change one's mind but to change one's ethos. The point of philosophy was to transform not just what we think but who we are.

One form of exercise was meditation. The word "meditation," Foucault noted, goes back through Latin to the Greek word *melete*.

> The Latin word *meditation* (or the verb *meditari*) translates the Greek substantive *melete*, the Greek verb *meletan*. This *melete*, this *meletan*, has a very different meaning from what we today, that is to say in the nineteenth and twentieth centuries, call "meditation." The *melete* is exercise.[12]

In modern languages, according to Foucault, *meditation* means primarily an intense concentration on some aspect of existence; it is not primarily a focused effort to deepen and develop a line of thought. "We think of meditation as an attempt to think of something with particular intensity without deepening its meaning, or letting our thought develop in a more or less regular order starting from the thing we are thinking about."[13] For the Greeks and Romans, however, meditation was different in two ways: to meditate on an insight was to incorporate it into our thinking so that it became "engraved in the mind" and "a principle of action"; and to meditate was also, through memory and imagination, to put oneself in the situation of a limit experience (loss, exile, sickness, and death) and to learn to see life from that perspective. In both ways, meditation is an effort to alter, deepen, clarify, and refine our understanding in order to move toward wisdom.

One form of meditation was writing. Writing for some philosophers was not just a means to preserve and communicate thought, Foucault argued, it was also a practice of meditation and an exercise of the soul. The point of writing was to move toward truth and, through that movement, to form or transform oneself.

> In whatever cycle of practice it takes place, writing constitutes an essential step in the process to which all askesis tends: to know the elaboration of received and recognized discourses as true in rational principles of action. As an element of the training of the self, writing has, to use an expression found in the writing of Plutarch, an *ethopoetic* function. It is an operator of transformation of truth into ethos.[14]

Meditative writing was understood as a practice through which one could make or remake one's ethos, according to Foucault: "It is his own soul that [the philosopher] must constitute as he writes."[15]

How can writing be a form of meditation? How can meditative writing let us move toward truth?

It is impossible to answer these questions if we take common concepts for granted. Language is not just a tool of communication, or means of self-expression, or a substitute for speaking, but also the medium in which we share a common understanding of the world. Thought does not just aim at knowledge, but aims to deepen, clarify, sharpen, complicate, and refine that common understanding. True understanding involves not just the correspondence of belief with reality, but the illumination of what has been hidden or dimly seen. Goodness is a matter not just of moral action, but also of the virtues that let one live a good life. Beauty is not just the sensible appearance of the ideal, or the pleasing qualities of aesthetic objects, but is also the shining appearance of the highest virtues. Inspiration is not taking dictation from a higher power, but an experience of revelation that enables us to create what we could not create through effort and craft alone. These common concepts reveal their limits when we use them to try to understand writing at its best. The experience of writing itself pushes us to rethink the nature of language, thought, truth, goodness, beauty, divinity, and wisdom.

But why pursue wisdom through writing? Isn't it possible simply to learn wisdom from others?

In the *Symposium*, Socrates laments that wisdom cannot be taught directly by one person to another.

> How good it would be, Agathon, if wisdom were the sort of thing that could flow out of the one of us who is fuller into him who is emptier, by our mere contact with each other, as water flows through wool from the fuller cup into the emptier.[16]

Why is wisdom unteachable? Knowledge can be taught. Information can be taught. Even practical skills can be taught. But wisdom cannot be taught, because it involves the way the world appears to us in light of our ethos. To move toward wisdom, we have to transform our ethos, and that means transforming everything that makes us who we are: our *vision* of the good; our *understanding* of things; our habitual *feelings*; the *languages* in which we think; the *practices* by which we live; the *ideals* we live for; our *virtues* and the *stories* of the *heroes* who embody them; our *values, temperament,* and *mores*; and the *formative experiences* in light of which we see the world.

This transformation is effected by work we do on ourselves, and one form of this work—one spiritual exercise—is meditative writing. In this sense, wisdom can only be approached through a kind of work that no one can do for us. In the words of Marcel Proust: "We do not receive wisdom, we must discover it for ourselves, after a journey through the wilderness that no one else can make for us, that no one can spare us, for our wisdom is the point of view from which we come at last to regard the world."[17]

But wisdom may also come as a gift—a grace that we receive from beyond ourselves, as we receive insight from inspiration. Yes, we must devote ourselves to the search for wisdom, and yes, that search requires the work of thought. But thought alone is not enough. To think is to reflect on experience, and experience has to be endured before and beyond all understanding. We learn to live by living. It is only through hard experience, and through reflecting on the meaning of that experience, that moments of truth come to us, and we come to see life in a new light. In the words of Aeschylus, "Zeus, who set us on the path to understanding, decreed that learning comes through suffering. Even in our sleep, pain recalled falls drop by drop into the heart until, against our will, from thrones on high, comes wisdom through the awful grace of gods."[18]

KINDS OF THOUGHT

WAYS OF THINKING

We started with a few theses. Writing is a way of thinking, but the link between thinking and writing clarifies nothing as long as the nature of thought remains unclear. The nature of thought is commonly misconceived in terms of a narrow conception of science: the sciences are reduced to methods of producing knowledge, and those methods are abstracted from their native sphere and read into the operations of the mind. This misconception privileges demonstrative thought at the expense of other kinds of thinking: interpretive thought, dialogical thought, and thinking in stories. The result is not just a narrow view of science, but a narrow view of thought itself.

But what are these four kinds of thought? What is demonstration? What is interpretation? What kind of thinking takes the form of dialogue? What does it mean to think in narrative? How are these kinds of thought different from each other, and how are they related?

DEMONSTRATION

Thinking is *demonstrative* when it aims to prove a definite thesis on the basis of logic and evidence.

One form of demonstrative thought ("*deduction*") starts from premises and lays out their logical consequences through a chain of inferences. The geometrical proofs of Euclid are classic examples of deduction, as is the argument of Jefferson in the Declaration of Independence, which deduces a right to revolution from a set of "self-evident" "truths." Deduction is also essential to empirical science—when scientists want to test a theory, they deduce what observable phenomena must exist if the theory is true, and then test the theory by looking to see if such phenomena can actually be observed.

Another form of demonstrative thought (in the broadest sense) is "*induction*," which starts from the facts of experience, discerns patterns in those facts, ventures a hypothesis to account for those patterns, revises or refines that hypothesis on the basis of further study, and finally lays down a thesis that tries to explain the facts through evidence and logical inference. Darwin's *Origin of Species* mimics the movement of induction.[1] Inductive arguments are not *logically* demonstrative, since their conclusions are based on particular facts that can never be definitively and certainly known. But they are demonstrative in the sense that they are essential to the sciences that aim to demonstrate claims on the basis of facts. Induction is the empirical work through which scientists formulate demonstrable theses.

A third form of demonstrative thought ("*reduction*") defines what something is by subtracting or "reducing" the traits that do not necessarily belong to it, in order to isolate a core set of necessary or "irreducible" traits that constitute what it is in essence. Descartes follows this path in *The Discourse on Method* when he tries to grasp what human beings are by subtracting all human traits that could be doubted until he is left with just one indubitable trait—thinking: "From this I knew that I was a substance, the whole essence or nature of which was merely to think."[2] Reduction in this sense tries to clarify the nature of things by subtracting from them everything that is inessential. This way of thinking is essential to modern science, which reduces beings to those traits that can be made reasonably clear and distinct.

Demonstrative thought aims at truths that can be known with certainty by any rational person. Such truths are supposed to be based on evidence alone. But evidence alone is never self-evident. In order for evidence to be seen *as* evidence of something, it has to be interpreted in terms of a basic understanding of what things are. Even the simplest empirical facts are ultimately grounded in assumptions that precede and guide empirical thought. It used to be a fact, for example, that the solar system had nine planets; scientists have now revised that number to eight, in light of a revised concept of what counts as a planet. Facts are never based on evidence alone, but always on evidence interpreted in light of a commonly accepted network of basic concepts. This means that demonstration always rests on a level of understanding that is not open to demonstration. Scientific proofs rest on assumptions that cannot be proven. Demonstrative thought is always grounded in and guided by a more basic level of thinking—the kind of thought concerned with interpretation.

INTERPRETATION

Thinking is *interpretive* when it aims to lay out the meaning of things, that is, to explicate the senses things have in the human world.

One form of interpretive thought is *exegesis*, which aims to clarify the meaning of a text by unpacking the significance of its words, by divining the intent of the author, or by making explicit the unspoken understanding of things implicit in the text. (The word *exegesis* means "leading out" or "bringing to light," and its opposite—*eisegesis* means reading *into* the text a meaning that is external to the text itself.) Biblical interpretation tends to be exegetical, in the sense that it aims through close reading to bring out the implicit meanings of written texts. And much literary thinking, even today, descends from traditions of Biblical exegesis.

A different kind of interpretive thought (*"critique of ideology"*) looks at things that are commonly seen as natural and universal and reinterprets them as the products of a particular society. This kind of critique tries to show that common interpretations are taken as true not because they correspond to natural realities, but because they serve the interests of those in power. Marx used this kind of thought in the *Communist Manifesto* to argue that while free markets are commonly interpreted as a natural part of human life, they are actually institutions produced by capitalist societies, and this interpretation of free markets is perpetuated not because it corresponds to reality, but because it serves the interests of the ruling class by obscuring the exploitation of workers.

Another kind of interpretive thought critiques inherited concepts in light of the way phenomena actually appear in experience. This way of thinking follows three steps: *Destruktion*: it lays out the terms in which a phenomenon is traditionally conceived and clarifies the sense of those terms by tracing them back to the experiences from which they were born; *Reduktion*: it looks at concrete examples of the phenomenon and asks what it is in essence; and *Konstruktion*: it locate the limits of traditional concepts by pointing to what eludes their grasp and then refines them in order to better grasp and illuminate what they have distorted or concealed. These three tasks define a way of thought ("*hermeneutic phenomenology*") that was laid out by Heidegger: "These three basic components of phenomenological method—reduction, construction, destruction—belong together in their content and must receive grounding in their mutual pertinence."[1]

Heidegger followed this path most clearly in "The Origin of the Work of Art." He first set out the terms in which art is traditionally conceived (*form* and *matter*), and traced those terms back to the experience from which they derive their original sense (the experience of forming products out of wood). He then described how a few works of art (a painting by van Gogh and a Greek temple) appear in experience and asked how these experiences might illuminate what art is in essence. Finally, he pointed out two traits in artworks that exceed the reach of traditional concepts (their power to illuminate the world and their resistance to final understanding) and rethought common words (*world* and *earth*) in order to name and grasp these traits as such.[2]

Hannah Arendt extended this path of thought in her political theory. In her essay *On Violence*, she first laid out inherited concepts of power and traced them back to the experience of domination; she then looked at the phenomenon of nonviolent revolution and asked how it illuminates the nature of power; and lastly, she argued that power, as it is traditionally conceived (power-over-others), depends on an overlooked but more basic level of power (the effective power-to-act of an organized group). This way of thought is central to her work as a whole. Her thinking is *interpretive* in the sense that it is ultimately grounded in "the critical interpretation of the past."[3]

But interpretive thought is never self-sufficient. Heidegger made this point in *Being and Time*: "Interpretation is never a presuppositionless grasping of something previously given."[4] Instead, interpretation is always grounded in a basic understanding of what things are. This basic understanding is the standpoint from which interpretation starts, which determines the way we approach what we aim to interpret, and which opens up a certain perspective. Every perspective lets us see some aspects of things clearly; it lets us see other aspects of things only at an angle and in a distorted way; and every perspective has blind spots—the side of things which that perspective does not let us see. Every standpoint also circumscribes a horizon of understanding—a space of clarity within which the world appears to us and beyond which phenomena do not even appear. Our horizon is the limit of our understanding. But this limit is never fixed. To move toward greater understanding is to move toward a higher standpoint, and this movement reveals what was hidden from our initial perspective and beyond the scope of our initial horizon. Different interpretations are always grounded in different standpoints that open up different approaches and offer different perspectives. So interpretive thought is always implicated in a deeper level of thinking—the kind of thought concerned with perspective.[5]

PERSPECTIVE

Thinking is *perspectival* insofar as it aims to clarify the insights, distortions, and blind spots of different points of view.

One kind of perspectival thought (*"dialogical"*) lays out a number of views, asks about their strengths and limitations, and tries to locate both their insights and their blind spots. Aeschylus thought dialogically in *The Eumenides,* where he laid out the views of justice held by Apollo and by the Furies, and where he tried to reconcile their opposing claims in the judgment of Athena.

Another kind of perspectival thought (*"demythification"*) lays out representations that claim to reflect reality as it is in itself, and then shows how these representations are actually partial and distorted images that show only the aspects of reality available to a particular point of view. Simone de Beauvoir used this kind of thought to argue that most literary images of women do not represent women as they really are, but only articulate the way women appear to men in sexist and patriarchal societies.[1]

A third kind of perspectival thought (*"genealogy"*) shows that words do not have meaning because they point directly to the timeless essences of beings. It shows instead that words have many senses, that these senses are bound to their history, and that these senses have shifted and mutated over time as the same words have been appropriated to name the ways things appear from radically different points of view. In *The Genealogy of Morals,* for example, Nietzsche argued that the ancient Greek word for "good"—*agathos*—meant something different in Homer than in the New Testament: in Homer *agathos* named the virtues that appear most worthy of honor from the perspective of a ruling warrior class; in the New Testament, *agathos* named the opposite virtues valorized by the very classes enslaved and oppressed in a society ruled by warriors. The point of genealogy, for Nietzsche, was not to elevate one perspective over another, for example, to celebrate the master morality of warriors and denounce the slave morality of the oppressed. Nor was it to merely juxtapose different perspectives without attempting to move beyond them. Instead, the point of genealogy was to reach a deeper understanding of morality by seeing it from more than one perspective.

> To see differently, to want to see differently, is no small discipline and preparation of the intellect for its future "objectivity"—the latter understood not as "contemplation without interest" (which is, as such, a nonconcept and an absurdity), but as having in our power our "pros" and "cons": so as to be able to engage and disengage them, so that we can use the difference in perspectives and affective interpretations

for knowledge [*so daß man sich gerade die verschiedenheit der Perspektiven und der Affekt-Interpretationen für die Erkenntnis nutzbar zu machen weiß.*].[2]

Note that Nietzsche does not reject the ideal of objectivity, but only criticizes a specific concept of objectivity that he takes to be shallow and misleading. His thinking aims to be objective, not in the sense that it offers us a view from nowhere, but in the sense that it engages and disengages with multiple perspectives in order to move toward a more multi-sided account of a topic. Genealogy does not claim that truth is relative to different perspectives; it explores different perspectives in order to move toward truth.

The truth of perspective is not just a matter of *correspondence* (correctness or rightness) but also a matter of *aletheia* (revelation or illumination). When we consider the truth of a perspective, we have to ask what it gets right: Does it offer a vision that accurately and fully corresponds to reality? But we also have to ask what it reveals and conceals: What does it let us see clearly? What does it let us see only in a distorted way? And what does it not let us see at all—what are blind spots proper to its point of view, and the horizon proper to its standpoint?

Perspectival thinking is dialogical, but in a way that goes beyond traditional concepts of dialogue. Dialogue is traditionally conceived as an exchange of views between people who share a common language—a language that is equally able to articulate both points of view. But our deepest disagreements involve differences for which there is no common language—radical differences of perspective articulated in languages between which there is no simple correspondence. Perspectival thinking at this level is a matter not just of considering other views within a single language, but learning the language of the other, learning to think in another language. To learn another language is to move away from our given standpoint toward a new standpoint that reveals what had been hidden from our given perspective and beyond the limits of our given horizon. This does not mean that we simply adopt the other's point of view and see the world from their perspective. Instead, we move toward a "higher" standpoint that expands our horizon and enables us to see what is visible from the other perspective that had been invisible from our own.[3]

The move from one perspective to another reveals the world in a new way, and this revelation occurs in time—it is an experience of illumination, a movement from blindness to insight. Because this movement occurs in time, it can only be understood in the form of a story. So perspectival thinking is never wholly self-sufficient; it must always rely on an even more basic and encompassing kind of thought—thinking in narrative.

NARRATION

In its simplest forms, narrative thought is grounded in the basic traits of human existence. Human beings are not just objects, who can be known by their objective traits, and not just subjects, who can be reduced to the contents of their consciousness. We are projects, in the sense that who we are now is a matter of both who we have been and who we might become.[1] To be human is to stand between past and future, and to know where I stand I have to know where I have come from and where I could go. As Charles Taylor has said, "making sense of my present action . . . requires a narrative understanding of my life, a sense of what I have become that can only be given in the form of a story . . . we understand ourselves inescapably in narrative."[2] To see people for who they are we have to understand their past and their possibilities—what history has made them, and what they could make of themselves. This understanding takes the form of a story.

But my story is never simply my own. To be human is to find oneself thrown into a world one has not chosen, and cast into dramas that began long before one was born.[3] We are born into possible ways of being (being a son or daughter, brother or sister, rich or poor, citizen or refugee), and we can choose other possibilities for ourselves (being a student, teacher, wife, mother, carpenter, artist, theist, atheist, or philosopher). In both cases, we understand both the past and the possibilities of human life in terms of stories that articulate the self-understanding of the communities into which we were born. We find ourselves in stories we have not written, and initially and for the most part, we understand ourselves in their terms.

These stories are meaningful, in the sense that they articulate the meanings of words, actions, events, and lives. Words are meaningful not just because they have definite senses, but because they can be used to point out and make visible phenomena in the world, and also because they reveal the character of the speaker. Actions are meaningful not just insofar as they aim at some good; they are also significant insofar as they follow a code, and they are revelatory insofar as they show the character of the one who acts. Events are meaningful insofar as they are explicable as part of a chain of causes and effects, and insofar as they may be subsumed under general concepts, but also insofar as they are so far beyond all foresight and preconception that they reveal how far reality exceeds our comprehension. Life itself is meaningful in several ways: in one sense, my life is meaningful insofar as it lives up to or falls short of ideals I share in common with others; in another sense, it is meaningful if I can grasp why it turned out the way it did. On the most basic level, my life is meaningful if I have something to live for. A meaningful life is oriented toward goods that make existence worthwhile; life seems meaningless when I have nothing to live for, when the goods of human life are utterly eclipsed.

To think in narrative is to try to understand the meanings of things through the construction of stories. "Construction" here means both construal and creation. To *construe* a story is to explicate the meanings of its words, actions, events, and lives. To *create* a story is to invent a sequence of these elements—words, actions, events, and lives—that brings them together in a way that brings out their meaning. Narrative thought is creative in the sense that it sheds new light on the world in which we live. But narrative thought is also interpretive in that it draws on the meanings that things always already have for us within the human world.

The nature of narrative thought has been distorted by scientistic concepts of self and world. For the sake of knowledge, modern science reduces the self to a subject and the world to objects devoid of meaning and worth. Within this perspective, it seems that we are each an isolated consciousness within a senseless universe, and that each of us must create meaning from scratch by inventing stories that make sense of what is senseless. This is a gross distortion of human existence. The realms of subjective experience and objective fact are grounded in a broader human world in which things always already have meaning and worth. Stories are one way in which we understand our existence within this broader world.

Narrative thinking aims at truth, but the truths it aims at are complex. On the most basic level, nonfiction narrative aims at truth in the sense of correspondence, in that it tries to get the facts right: the truth, the whole truth, and nothing but the truth. But a factually accurate narrative can still be untrue in the sense that it selects facts in a way that distorts or conceals the real story. A good nonfiction narrative selects precisely the facts that reveal and illuminate the essence of what really happened.

Fictional narrative aims at truth in another sense: it suspends the concern for factual truth in order to capture essential truth. Think of Plato's allegory of the cave—the story is untrue in the sense that it is pure fiction, but the fiction aims to capture the essence of education. Think also of the parable of the Prodigal Son—the story is a fiction, but a fiction that aims to illuminate the nature of sin and love. Or think of Proust's great novel—it is (among other things) a narrative that aims to illuminate the nature of art. Stories at their best aim at truth as illumination.

KINDS OF WRITING

PAPERS

The form of a text should follow from its aim. Texts that aim at demonstration tend to be organized around a thesis—a claim the writer tries to show is true on the basis of evidence and argument. Most thesis-driven papers follow a conventional form.

1. The first paragraph introduces a topic and sets down a thesis.
2. Several supporting paragraphs lay out evidence for the thesis.
3. Later paragraphs may lay out and refute counterarguments.
4. A concluding paragraph summarizes the argument.

This form is best for arguments based on facts, such as scientific papers, legal arguments, and letters of recommendation.

If the paper is written for people who are busy or distracted, it's best to state the thesis in the very first sentence, and then elaborate that statement in the rest of the paper, starting with its most important aspects and introducing refinements, subtleties, and implications later on.

Thesis-driven writing has its virtues: it pushes us to ground our beliefs on evidence, to rethink our beliefs if the evidence does not fit our preconceptions, to ground generalizations in specific examples, and to articulate ideas in a clear and persuasive way.

But it also has its weaknesses. It steers writers away from questions that cannot be answered on the basis of evidence. It makes writing for oneself seem like a moot exercise. It pushes us to approach texts not as partners in a dialogue, but as witnesses in a controlled interrogation whose purpose is to gather evidence in order to prove a case.

The thesis-driven paper is commonly taught in writing courses precisely because it articulates the most common kind of critical thought—thought that suspends trust in one's beliefs in order to see if they are logically coherent and grounded in the best available evidence. But just as there are other kinds of thought, so there are other kinds of writing.

ESSAYS

It helps to distinguish *papers* from *essays*.

Papers aim at knowledge. The writer has done research on a topic and uses the paper to report that research and to make a claim to impersonal truth—truth that is based on evidence and argument whose validity is independent of the writer's personal views.

Essays are attempts at understanding. The writer uses the act of writing to work out her own insights—to open up a path of thought that reaches a new point of view. This point of view offers a glimpse of truth—an understanding that is deep, clear, precise, complex, and refined. The truth of an essay is personal, in the sense that it draws on the writer's own experience and place in the world, and yet it is a truth that is open to anyone who can follow the writer's line of thought.

Essays are more conducive to meditative writing. They start with a question and lead step by step toward an answer. The answer is the writer's thesis, but the thesis appears at the end of the essay rather than the start.

One can start an essay with a question, but questions don't come out of nowhere—a true question articulates the wonder we feel when we encounter something that strikes us and yet resists or eludes understanding. So an essay may also introduce a question by pointing to something obscure—a story, quotation, paradox, puzzle, mystery, apparent contradiction, or counterintuitive fact. The point of such an introduction is to lead readers into the sense of wonder articulated by the question.

Question-driven essays have a conventional form:

1. The first section introduces and/or poses a question.
2. The next sections may summarize one or two ways in which the question is commonly answered.
3. The essay then introduces a relevant text.
4. It lays out a reading of the text by quoting and explicating key passages that are relevant to the question.
5. In light of this reading, it may show how common answers to the question are inadequate.
6. In the end, it lays out the writer's own answer to the question.

This form is flexible. If the central question is simple, it can be asked at the very start of the essay. More complicated questions need to be introduced and can go in the middle or even near the end of an essay.

The question-driven form is conducive to meditative writing for several reasons:

Starting with a question pushes us to focus on the limits of our comprehension and to recognize that something eludes, resists, or exceeds our grasp—something that needs to be more clearly, precisely, and fully understood. By giving us the task of leading readers step by step from a lesser to a greater degree of understanding, it encourages us to move toward greater understanding through the process of writing itself.

Question-driven essays also force us to better understand the texts we quote. Both thesis-driven and question-based essays include quotations from other texts, but the *function* of the quotations is different in each. A thesis-driven paper tends to approach a text as an interrogator approaches a witness—the point of the quotations is to provide evidence to build a case. A question-based essay tends to approach a text as a thinker approaches a partner in a dialogue— the point of the quotations is to explicate and clarify the insights implicit in the text, and to critically appropriate those insights in order to reach a new level of understanding.

Question-driven essays let us write about *essential* questions (questions about what things are in essence) that cannot be answered on the basis of evidence, since they concern the prior understanding that guides how we interpret and evaluate evidence.

Since question-driven essays aim at a better understanding of a question through a dialogue with another text, they help us see writing as a way to clarify, deepen, and refine our own thoughts.

DIALOGUES

The search for wisdom is bound to ask essential questions: What is truth? What is goodness? What is beauty? What is wisdom? These are true questions only if we suspend all claim to already know the answers. In the words of Augustine, "Let none of us say he has already found the truth. Let us look for it as though we did not yet know it on either side; for we can search for it in peace and devotion only if both parties, rejecting all presumptuous prejudice, renounce the belief that it is already found and known."[1] This suspension of certainty is essential to a genuine search, and since Plato, the search for wisdom has primarily taken the form of dialogue.

Dialogues are perspectival. Every perspective has strengths and limits: it lets us see some aspects of the world clearly, some aspects in a distorted way, and some aspects not at all. Dialogues stage a clash of perspectives in order to explore their insights, distortions, and blind spots.

Perspective is grounded in character. Character means ethos—the way of being in the world that underlies our point of view. So each character in a dialogue should speak out of lived experience, and out of the ethos that governs his or her life. Good characters articulate distinctive points of view, and good dialogue brings together profoundly different characters: Socrates and Thrasymachus; St. Francis and Saladin; the Dude and the Big Lebowski; King Arthur and Dennis the Peasant.

Character is revealed in discourse. The people in a dialogue reveal their ethos not just in what they say but in how they say it. So the voice of each character should be distinct. In simple dialogues, the characters have different views but share a common language in which those views can be expressed. In more complex dialogues, the characters may lack a common language and describe their differences in different terms. Aeschylus dramatized this depth of difference in *The Oresteia*: Apollo and the Furies not only have different views of justice, they cannot even agree on what to call the act for which Orestes is on trial. Their disagreement includes the different kinds of discourse proper to different ethea.

Dialogue means *talking through* (*dia*, "through," and *legein*, "to talk"). Essential to a philosophical dialogue is that characters talk through a question in order to move toward an understanding that none of them has in advance.

We talk through a question by exploring different perspectives. Each character tentatively responds to the question and gives examples that show the grain of truth in his or her response. Other characters can then point out the weaknesses in the example or offer counterexamples that push them all to refine the given answer or to offer tentative answers of their own. The point is to test the strengths and weaknesses of several points of view: What does each view let us see clearly? What does it show us only in a distorted way? And what does it wholly obscure?[2]

Essential questions don't come from nowhere. They often follow from concrete questions that arise from an impasse or *aporia*, when reality baffles the terms in which we think, and we don't know how to think or what to do. Sometimes these concrete questions are retrospective, as in *The Oresteia*, where the question of justice follows from the concrete question of whether Orestes was right to kill his mother. Sometimes these concrete questions are prospective, as in the *Crito*, where the question of justice follows from the concrete question of whether Socrates should try to escape from jail. In both cases, an aporia raises a concrete question for the characters, and the concrete question raises the essential question at the center of the dialogue.

The link between concrete and essential questions may be laid out in a *backstory*, which frames the dialogue and highlights what is at stake in its outcome. The stakes may be laid out in a story that frames the dialogue, or they may be revealed in a story that emerges within the dialogue itself. In a drama, the stakes should be as high as possible. In a comedy, there should be the greatest possible disjunction between the gravity of the philosophical stakes and the triviality of the external stakes. The function of the framing story is to show how the question at the center of the dialogue arises in experience and to show how this question is related to the fundamental question of how to live.

So dialogues tend to have a classic structure:

1. A backstory that frames the dialogue.
2. An impasse or *aporia* that baffles common ways of thought.
3. A concrete question raised by the aporia.
4. An essential question raised by the concrete question.
5. (a) A first answer, with arguments and examples.
   (b) Counterexamples and counterarguments.
6. (a) A second answer, with arguments and examples.
   (b) Counterexamples and counterarguments.
7. Further answers and counterarguments.
8. Conclusion.

Dialogues may conclude in several ways. They may offer a final answer that synthesizes the insights in all the preceding answers. They may end in wonder, as many Platonic dialogues do, with the characters perplexed and ready once again to start talking through the essential question. Or they may end with an irresolvable conflict between two irreconcilable perspectives. (René Girard has argued that the dialogues in the Book of Job aim to reveal just such a clash of perspectives: "Of all the revelatory details offered by the Book of Job, the most extraordinary remains the counterpoint of the two perspectives, made possible by the dialogue format".)[3]

But even dialogues that are inconclusive aim at truth, in that they aim to bring to light and illuminate the blind spots or contradictions hidden in common ways of thought. The truth of dialogue is not a matter of certainty, but of making manifest what has been overlooked or concealed. In the words of David Tracy (again): "Conversation accords primacy to one largely forgotten notion of truth: truth as manifestation . . . . Without genuine conversation, no manifestation. Without manifestation, no real dialogue."[4]

STORIES

Storytelling is a way of thinking. And thinking in narrative, according to Hannah Arendt, can be more illuminating than conceptual thought: "No philosophy, no analysis, no aphorism, be it ever so profound, can compare in intensity and richness of meaning with a properly narrated story."[1]

Just as there are many ways of thinking in narrative, so there are many kinds of narrative discourse: myth, fable, parable, allegory, epic, testimony, tale, memoir, biography, history, genealogy, and so on. Let us look at just four forms of narrative that are especially conducive to the search for wisdom.[2]

The simplest is *testimony*. Testimonies are essential to the effort to understand what things are on the basis of the way they appear in experience. They are especially important for phenomena that lie beyond the scope of common experience, such as slavery, combat, prison, and tyranny; in these cases, testimony makes real what we can barely imagine, conveys the shock and horror of events, and helps to ground our thinking in reality as it is revealed in experience. But testimony is also important for phenomena that lie within the scope of common experience but beyond the reach of ordinary discourse, such as Proust's accounts of involuntary memory. In these cases, if testimony adheres to experience with sufficient care and precision, it can be a source of truth before and beyond conceptual thought. Merely by narrating experiences that have remained sunk in the subverbal regions of human life, writers can bring to light and illuminate phenomena that have been obscurely felt but never recognized as such.

A second kind of narrative is the *public story*.[3] Public stories aim at political persuasion in two ways: they aim to lead an audience step by step to share a point of view; and they aim to convey the emotions that will inspire the audience to take action. Emotions show us what matters—to be effective, public stories have to be both lucid and passionate: lucid enough to offer a clear view of our situation, the challenges we face, and a realistic path forward; and passionate enough to call us back to what really matters and to inspire us to work together for the common good.

Public stories argue for a specific course of action by approaching a political issue through a personal narrative, then by situating that personal narrative in a larger history, and finally using that history to chart a path forward. So they tend to have a three-part structure.

The first part of a public story is a personal narrative. It narrates how you came to care about a political issue. This story has to lay out where you have come from, what you have done, the challenges you have faced, the choices you made, the obstacles you have handled, and above all the specific experiences that led you to see a political issue as you now do. The point of this section is to lead your audience step by step through the experiences that led you to your point of view.

The second part of a public story situates your personal story in a larger history. You may use facts and statistics to show that your own experience is part of a larger story. But facts alone are not compelling. What matters in this part is to shift the focus of the story from "I" to "we"—to shift from speaking as an individual to speaking as part of a community that includes the audience. Show the audience how their own lives are implicated in the story you tell.

The third part of a public story is a call to action. A good call to action charts a path from where we have been, and where we are now, to where we should go. It articulates an affirmative vision for the future, but it also lays out simple, realistic, concrete, achievable actions that can move us toward that future, actions that appeal to the broadest possible coalition and that rectify the most flagrant and obvious injustices. Gandhi articulated a grand vision of India free of colonial rule, for example, but he first proposed more humbly that Indians make their own salt in order to pressure the British to rescind the salt tax. The ultimate point of politics is not just to "raise consciousness," but to persuade people to work together to get things done. Public stories are most effective when they chart a path from present problems to a better future through specific, concrete, and achievable actions.

So public stories have a conventional three-part structure:

1. The Story of You.
   (a) Where have you come from?
   (b) What have you done?
   (c) What challenges have you faced?
   (d) What experience has led you to your view of a political problem?
   (e) What story most clearly shows the nature of the problem?
2. The Story of Us.
   (a) What is the larger history of which your story is a part?
   (b) How has that history led to the situation we are in today?
   (c) What is the basic problem that we have to solve?
3. The Story of Now.
   (a) What concrete action can move us toward that solution?
   (b) How does that action affirm the goods to which we are devoted?
   (c) What are the goods that make life meaningful and worth living?

Public stories are suited to political discourse, since people think about politics in narrative. Political discourse does contain elements of demonstrative thought—facts, data, evidence, logic, and theory—but these elements are meaningless if they are not situated in a story that speaks to people's sense of what really matters. This does not mean that in politics we should abandon demonstrative thought, but it does mean we should abandon narrow and superficial views of political discourse. Our political discourse will be both more illuminating and more effective if it uses all the resources of narrative thought.

A third kind of narrative thought is the *transition story*—a first-person story that narrates a movement from blindness to insight, from a lesser to a greater understanding. Such stories have a conventional structure, in three acts:

The first act of a transition story lays out a past blindness. Usually, blindness is a matter not of total ignorance but of taking for granted views that are shallow, confused, vague, simplistic, and crude. And usually, these views are not really our own; they are the views we have thoughtlessly absorbed from people around us. The first act of a transition story aims to present the essential traits of this myopia. In a first-person story, the first act tries to say what I believed, to give the flimsy and superficial reasons why this belief seemed to make sense, to describe the error to which I was opposed, in contrast to which my view seemed completely true, to mark the limits of my vision by explaining what I could never understand, and to articulate the biased and self-serving explanations I accepted for why other people thought differently. The first act may also explore why I was bound to this myopia: the bond I felt with the people who shared this view, my admiration for the person who passed it on to me, my commitment to the ethos from which this belief seemed inseparable, the story I told myself, the self-image to which I was attached, and the states of the soul (pride, envy, anger, sloth, greed, gluttony, or lust) that clouded my vision. Blindness is rarely just a matter of incorrect belief; more often it is the skewed view and narrow horizon proper to a particular standpoint. The first act of the story describes the blindness proper to a point of view.

The second act of a transition story tells how this view became untenable. Here the focus must be on specific experiences. The second act of a first-person story may focus on an event that baffled my expectations; an encounter that eluded my comprehension; a journey that took me past familiar horizons; a situation I could not have imagined; an episode that made no sense within the story I told myself; a person who saw the world from another point of view, or who led me to see myself through different eyes; a conversation that called into question what I had taken for granted; a book that exposed me to a different way of thought; a work of art that made real what had seemed abstract; my having to deal with something that eluded familiar ways of thought. These experiences may have inspired wonder, but the second act of the story shows how I articulated that wonder in misguided questions—questions that presupposed bogus assumptions and that were framed in crude and inadequate terms. The point of the second act is to lay out the conditions under which—without reaching any new insight—I started to sense the limits of my view, to mistrust the explanations I held, to feel unease where I had once felt at home, to intuit something whose essence escaped the terms in which I tried to grasp it. The function of every element in the second part is to set up the transition that occurs in the third act.

The third act of a transition story narrates a transition from blindness to insight. These movements are complex because blindness is complex: I tend to be not just ignorant, but unaware of my own ignorance. So transitions tend to happen in at least two steps. The first step toward insight is to see my blindness as such. Usually, there is a decisive moment when reality reveals how far it exceeds my powers of comprehension, and the distance between thought and reality becomes too great to ignore. My assumptions collapse; my discourse breaks down; my self-image implodes. I am forced to face the limits of my understanding. The second step is a moment of truth: I move away from my old standpoint, and this movement expands my horizon and shifts my view so that what had been hidden is more fully revealed. But this revelation is rarely complete. Instead of complete understanding, I am left with the sense that what I can now understand is much less than what remains to be understood.

So transition stories have a classic form. Ask yourself:

1. The blindness of a past view.

    (a) What view did I hold?

    (b) What were the grounds that seemed to support it?

    (c) What was the error to which I was opposed?

    (d) What were the bonds that bound me to that perspective?

    (e) What from that perspective could I never understand?

2. The experiences that called that view into question.

    (a) What event baffled my expectations?

    (b) What person eluded my preconceptions?

    (c) What artworks and books challenged how I thought?

3. The movement from blindness to insight.

    (a) When did I start to recognize my blindness?

    (b) What was the moment of truth?

    (c) When was I able to see further horizons to be explored?

The clearest example of this structure is Tolstoy's novella, *The Death of Ivan Ilyich*, which has twelve chapters: the first four chapters lay out the blindness of the hero; the second four chapters show how this blindness gradually becomes untenable; and the last four chapters show the sequence of revelations through which he moves toward wisdom. The same structure is implicit in some of the greatest life stories ever written: Augustine's *Confessions*; Tolstoy's *Confession*; and Proust's *In Search of Lost Time*.

A transition story of this kind makes a claim to truth, since it narrates a movement from blindness to insight. But the truth it claims is not final or definitive; it merely claims that I ended up closer to truth than where I was at the start.

The conventions of transition stories are not arbitrary; they are grounded in basic ways of thinking in narrative. We tend to think about how to live in terms of stories about transitions—movements from error to truth, confusion to clarity, blindness to insight, worse to better ways of being. Charles Taylor has laid out this argument most clearly: "This is, I believe, the commonest form of practical reasoning in our lives, where we propose to our interlocutors *transitions* mediated by such error-reducing moves, by the identification of a contradiction, the dissipation of confusion, or by rescuing from (usually motivated) neglect a consideration whose significance they cannot contest."[4] This genre of narrative discourse is not an arbitrary invention, but the articulation in words of a distinct kind of narrative thought.

A fourth kind of narrative is the *life story*. Life stories are the most conducive to the search for wisdom, but they are also the hardest to write. How to write the story of one's life?

This question is usually answered in three ways. Each answer offers a distinctive approach to telling a life story, and each approach is grounded in a distinctive view of the self. To work out our own answer to the question, we have to understand each approach, the strengths and limitations of its view of the self, and the way it illuminates or distorts the story of a life.

The first approach views the self as an *object* of knowledge. This is the approach of obituaries and encyclopedias, which focus only on the facts, but also the main approach of biographies and autobiographies, which start with the facts and try to explain their underlying causes. A life story, in this view, is a sequence of incidents held together by a chain of causes and effects. In the words of George Saunders: "that's really all a story is: a series of things that happens in sequence, in which we can discern a pattern of causality . . . causation is what creates the appearance of meaning."[5] To write my life story in this way is to search for self-knowledge, where knowledge means the causal explanation of objective facts.

This approach has its strengths. Facts are essential to the search for truth—they are the points of contact with reality that resist our delusions and bind us to what is real. A narrative of a life is not true, in the most basic sense, if it does not correspond to objective reality. If our lives hold any truth, we approach that truth only by an interpretation of the facts.

But this approach also has its limits. We can be reduced to objective traits and understood objectively *to some extent*, but human beings are not just objects. Explanation is a limited mode of understanding: concepts of cause and effect, which are rooted in the experience of nonhuman beings, necessarily fail to grasp the essential elements of human histories—the spontaneity of free action and the novelty of unprecedented events—and so are bound to distort the story of any human life.[6] Above all, truth is not simply a matter of fact. Facts are meaningful only when they signify deeper truths, and their significance is always a matter of interpretation. Without this work of interpretation, a life story is bound to miss the essential.

A second approach views the self as a *subject*. It focuses on the subjective experience of the writer, as filtered through the writer's memory, and it lays out a narrative of a consciousness from first memories to the present. In particular, such writing focuses on precise descriptions of the sensory qualities of things—the feel, look, sound, smell, and taste of things. At its most extreme, the aim of such writing is simply to offer the reader a vicarious version of the writer's own experience, to capture the particulars of life in their pure particularity. To write my life story in this way is to trace the history of my consciousness.

This approach has its strengths. Even if life writing aims only at the particular, it may still be a source of truth if it describes phenomena beyond the horizon of common experience, or brings to light experiences that have remained in the shadows of pre-verbal life. And even if our ultimate aim is essential truth, we have to start from reality as it is revealed in personal experience.

But this approach also has its limits. The more a story focuses on the subjectivity of the writer, the more it overlooks the human worlds we share with others, in which things have a common meaning and worth. It is a mistake to understand life starting from the consciousness of a worldless subject, as Heidegger argued in *Being and Time*: "a mere subject without a world 'is' not initially and is also never given." "The world is always already the one I share with others."[7] If we try to understand life starting from the experience of subjectivity, it will seem as if the task of the writer is to invent meaning within a meaningless universe, and the story itself will have no meaning except that bestowed by the writer. At worst, such a life story devolves into a tedious chronicle of subjective experiences important to the writer alone. But stories can do more. A good story aims at meaning beyond subjective significance.

A third approach views the self as a *being in the world*. Such a story situates my own life in the broader life of the world in which I live. This approach to writing aims not just to portray the realities of human nature, but to illuminate the possibilities of human existence. Milan Kundera laid out this view of narrative in his thoughts on the novel. "A novel examines not reality but existence. And existence is not what has occurred, existence is the realm of human possibilities, everything that man can become, everything he's capable of. Novelists draw up *the map of existence* by discovering this or that human possibility. But again, to exist means 'being-in-the-world.'"[8] What Kundera says of the novel here applies to any life story. A life story may be not merely a record of what occurred, but also an exploration of existence. The aim may be not just to portray the reality of the past, but to illuminate the possibilities of human life—not just to record what has been but to show us what we can be.

The great strength of this approach is that it recognizes the basic problem of the life writer: Our lives have been full of meaning—significant words, decisive actions, revelatory events—but we don't yet fully understand what that meaning is. We are born into a world of meanings that we share in common with others, and we have come to see ourselves in light of that common understanding, but our self-understanding (again) is flawed in two ways: on the one hand, it is *average* (i.e., relatively shallow, confused, vague, simplistic, and crude); on the other hand, it is mostly *inauthentic* (i.e., passively absorbed and thoughtlessly taken for granted). The aim of life writing, in this approach, is not just to accurately portray the past or to lay out an understanding that I have already achieved, but to meditate on my life in order to reach a better understanding of the meaning of my experience. Better in two senses: both more *genuine*, in the sense that in the process of writing my understanding becomes deeper, clearer, more precise, complex, and refined; and also more *authentic*, in the sense that through writing I work toward an understanding that is more fully my *own*.

The great weakness of this approach is that its ultimate point is not clear. Yes, we can draw up a map of human existence. But why? For the sake of what? To what end?

These three approaches to life writing all have value—they each let us see an aspect of the self and tell the story of one side of a life. But each is one-sided, and all together they still miss what is essential.

A fourth approach to life writing views the self as a *project*. The self is a project in the sense that we are always in motion in two dimensions.

First, we are always moving from past to future. To be human is to be in motion from what we have been toward what we could be. We have to recognize this motion in order to see people for who they are. This is clear in the case of children—we understand who they are now in light of who they might become. But this is also true of self-understanding—I always see who I am now in light of where I have come from and what I aim to be, how I have lived and how I want to live. To understand who someone is, we have to know their story.[9] We can think of this as the *horizontal* dimension of human existence: we are always moving away from the past and forward into the future.

Second, we are moved by what we see as good. The good exerts a force of attraction on us that moves us to act. This is obviously true when goodness simply means pleasure, and it is clearly true where the good means the useful. But this is also true in an ethical sense, where the good means what is most worthy of love and respect—what is beautiful in the sense of the word *kalos*. This attraction to the good is a basic trait of human beings. In the words of Charles Taylor: "the notion of the self . . . is meant to pick out this crucial feature of human agency, that we cannot do without some orientation to the good, that we each essentially are . . . where we stand on this."[10] To be human is not just to want to *have* what is good, but to want to *be* good, that is, to aspire to be something higher than we are now. We can think of this as the *vertical* dimension of human existence: we are always trying to move upwards toward some vision of the good.

This vision of the good is what gives life *meaning*. Things are meaningful to us insofar as they are relevant to what we are living for. If I live for pleasure, as Epicurus did, then the finest distinctions between different kinds of pleasure will become profoundly meaningful. If I decide that pleasure is irrelevant to a good life, as Marcus Aurelius did, then these fine distinctions will appear meaningless. The link between goodness and meaning was clearly described by Tolstoy in his life story, *A*

Confession. In the early chapters, he described "those strivings for goodness which lent meaning to my life" when he was young. In the middle chapters, he described how spiritual life became meaningless to him when he devoted himself to worldly goods, and how worldly life later became meaningless when he devoted himself once more to the goods of the spirit: "the life of our class, the rich and learned, not only became distasteful to me, but lost all meaning." In the later chapters, he described how he "returned to a belief in God, in moral perfection, and to that tradition that had given life a meaning."[11] What matters, in this context, is not the content of Tolstoy's belief but the link that he described between meaning and our vision of the good. We understand ourselves and the world in light of the good. Our vision of the good is essential to our vision of ourselves. Self-understanding is irreducibly ethical, in the sense that it is rooted in our ethos. Our ethos is constitutive of our self. We do not *have* an ethos; we *are* an ethos.

The two movements of the self as a project—horizontal motion through time, vertical motion toward the good—give human life the form of a quest. This quest is often figured as an uphill struggle: we move forward into the future in order to move upward toward the highest good. Think of Plato's allegory of the cave, or Dante's ascent from the lowest state of the soul to the highest. For Plato and Dante, this quest is the basic plot of any life story. Alasdair MacIntyre made explicit what is implicit in these allegories when he wrote that, "The unity of a human life is the unity of a narrative quest."[12]

The quest for a good life is also a quest for truth. But this quest is often misconceived. It does not aim at truth for its own sake, but at truth for the sake of a good life. People do not naturally want every kind of knowledge; they want the kind of understanding that is conducive to living well. To live well we have to see things for what they are, and to see clearly the goods that make existence worthwhile. So our quest for truth is not primarily motivated by love of learning (*philomathia*) but by love of wisdom (*philosophia*). All human beings are lovers of wisdom. The quest for wisdom is built into the structure of human existence.

Needless to say, this quest always goes wrong. The essential components of any life story are blindness, myopia, error, descent, failure, disappointment, pain, suffering, despair, reversals, and occasional moments of truth. No honest life story is an unbroken record of wisdom and success. The implicit subtitle of any true life story is: *How I Tried to Live a Good Life, Why I Mostly Failed, and What I Came to See Along the Way.*

Think of Augustine. Tolstoy. Proust. Their life stories are a sequence of transition stories, which focus mostly on the illusions they held, the errors into which they fell, the dead ends they went down in their misguided pursuit of happiness, the suffering they endured, the despair they felt in going astray, the darkness of the world when every higher good is eclipsed. And they also narrate the reversals of direction, the gradual climb out of the depths, and the moments of truth that led them to the point from which they write. The turning points of their stories are the shifts in their vision of the good, the changes in what they were living for, the moments when a higher good was revealed, in whose light the world appeared more clearly, in which they appeared more clearly to themselves. It was these moments of truth that pushed them to rethink their whole past, and they accomplished that rethinking by writing their life story.

This kind of life writing is a spiritual exercise. It is a meditation on experience that aims at wisdom.

Life stories are the kind of writing most conducive to the search for wisdom, but whatever wisdom we manage to reach through our writing will be communicated not by propositions but by the virtues of the writing itself: the charity with which we portray others, the justice we do to those who have hurt us, the courage with which we face painful truths, the temperance with which we resist self-indulgent scribbling, the thoughtfulness of our diction, the quality of attention implicit in our descriptions, the insight of our wit, the candor with which we face our failures and the humility we show toward what we still don't understand. The wisdom in a life story is not conveyed in maxims and *bon mots*; it is conveyed by how our writing illuminates human existence.

No need to fully understand your life before you start writing; the discipline of writing itself will lead to understanding. Start with the stories of people who matter to you, testimony about your formative experiences, and transition stories about turning points in your life. Do justice to the triumphs, joys, and moments of truth. But be honest about illusions, errors, dead ends, suffering, darkness, and moments of despair. Keep in mind the questions of Augustine, Tolstoy, and Proust: How have I tried to live a good life? How have I failed? And what have I come to see along the way?

Set aside a little time every day to write in search of wisdom. In the words of Epicurus:

> Let no one be slow to seek wisdom when he is young, nor weary of the search when he is old. For no age is too early or too late for the health of the soul. And to say that you are too young or too old to do philosophy is like saying you are too young or too old for happiness. So both old and young should seek wisdom, the former so that, as age comes over them, they may be young in blessings, through the joy of what has been, and the latter in order that, while they are young, they may at the same time be old, because they have no fear of what is to come. So we must practice the things that bring happiness.[13]

To write in search of wisdom is to blaze a path of thought.

PRINCIPLES OF COMPOSITION

PRINCIPLES

Some of the dullest books ever written are books on writing, and they are dull because they are devoid of thought. Instead of laying out thoughts on writing, they dictate rules on how to write. H. L. Mencken saw this clearly:

> With precious few exceptions, all books on style in English are by writers quite unable to write. The subject, indeed, seems to exercise a special and dreadful fascination over school ma'ams, bucolic college professors, and other such pseudoliterates. . . . Their central aim, of course, is to reduce the whole thing to a series of simple rules—the overmastering passion of their melancholy order, at all times and everywhere.[1]

Mencken is right: Rules are no substitute for experience, intelligence, skill, taste, judgment, knowledge, wit, and wisdom. All the rules in the world can't take the place of hard, daily, deliberate practice. In the end, we learn to write by writing.

Still, it helps to have some guidance when starting out. New writers need rules distilled from experience, at least at first. But the more they practice writing and reflect on their practice, the more they will understand writing at a level of depth and complexity beyond anything that can be grasped by general rules.[2]

We need rules to get to the point where we don't need rules.

Process

1. Give yourself time.
2. Read and write at the same time.
3. Write multiple drafts.
4. Get feedback on each draft.
5. Write until you can say the same thing in brief and at length.
6. Proofread your penultimate draft.

Outline

7. Use the order of your text to show the order of your subject.
8. Make outlines.
9. Lay out paragraphs in a coherent sequence of steps.
10. Start by indicating the subject right away.

Argument

11. Give your readers what they need to follow your argument.

12. Put in your argument only what is relevant to your point.
13. If you make more than two points, enumerate them.
14. Find the grains of truth in other views.
15. Do justice to views you think are wrong.

Questions

16. Use questions to introduce topics.
17. Prepare your readers for difficult questions.

Examples

18. Use regular examples to relate the specific to the general.
19. Use counterexamples to show the limits of common views.
20. Choose examples that show the importance of your point.

Quotations

21. Do justice to the works you quote.
22. Incorporate quotations in a grammatically coherent way.

23. Don't put long quotations in the middle of a sentence.

24. Make sure the sense and context of quotations are clear.

25. Put short quotations into quotation marks.

26. Set off long quotations in indented and single-spaced blocks.

Paragraphs

27. Focus each paragraph on just *one* topic.

28. Organize each paragraph around a topic sentence.

29. Place key sentences in a paragraph at the start or the end.

30. Create continuity within paragraphs by carrying over key words from one sentence to the next.

31. Create continuity between paragraphs with parallel topic sentences.

32. Don't overuse the same paragraph structure.

33. Keep verb tenses consistent.

Sentences

34. Be concise.

35. Use simple sentences to emphasize general points.

36. Use complex sentences to show relations between several points.

37. Articulate related ideas in similar sentence structures.

38. Don't overuse the same sentence structure.

39. Keep related words together.

40. Put the emphatic words of a sentence at the end.

41. Use active and passive verbs wherever they fit best.

42. Avoid extended compound subjects.

Words

43. Be precise.

44. Use the simplest appropriate word.

45. Use technical terms only if you know what they mean.

46. Introduce technical terms by explaining them in plain English.

47. Don't mix dead metaphors.

48. Use figurative language judiciously.

49. Avoid turning verbs into nouns.

50. Speak to others in a language they can understand.

PROCESS

1. Give Yourself Time

The time of writing is different from the time of daily life. In daily life, our time is not free: we have to work, to meet obligations, to deal with the demands of the moment and with situations that call on us to act. We focus on the ephemeral and lose sight of what really matters.

To regain perspective, we have to give ourselves time to write—to step away from daily life, to come back to ourselves, to reconnect with our deeper concerns, to gather thoughts, to try to see things for what they are, and to put what we see into words. Writing every day is both a discipline and a form of devotion: it is the long, slow work of moving toward true understanding, and also a gift of time devoted to what we love.

Think of Marcus Aurelius. He gave himself time to write, even when he was Emperor of Rome, because writing for him was a way to strengthen his soul. In the words of Pierre Hadot, "As he wrote the *Meditations,* Marcus was thus practicing Stoic spiritual exercises . . . . This was an exercise of writing day by day, ever-renewed, always taken up again and always needing to be taken up again, since the true philosopher is he who is conscious of not yet having attained wisdom."[1] If Marcus could find time to write, then so can you.

Writing takes time. To do it well takes more time than you think. Don't tell yourself you will get around to writing at some point in the future. The time to write is now.

2. Read and Write at the Same Time

Don't separate reading and writing. Seneca made this point in a letter to a friend: "We ought neither to write exclusively nor read exclusively: the first—writing, that is—will deaden and exhaust our powers; the second will weaken and dilute them. One must do both by turns, tempering one with the other, so that whatever is collected through reading may be assimilated into the body by writing."[2] It is a mistake to think that *first* we do the work of reading, and *afterwards* do the work of writing.

To *read* a text well, it helps to start writing about it: highlight key sentences, use post-it notes to tag significant passages, make comments in the margins, write out notes on crucial parts of the text, and jot down ideas you want to include in your writing. If you deeply admire a text, copy its key passages word for word. Just copying a text will help you learn its style.

To *write* well about a text, it helps to go back and re-read it; nothing makes us read a text more carefully than having to write about it. Start writing while you are reading, and go back and re-read while you are writing.

3. Write Multiple Drafts

Good writing takes rewriting. Nothing great was written in one draft. Tolstoy wrote six full drafts of *Anna Karenina*. Elie Wiesel's first draft of *Night* was 862 pages, which he eventually cut down to 116. On each draft, do the best you can in the time you have. Then rewrite ruthlessly: rethink the outline, reorganize the paragraphs, cut the clutter, polish the language.

A rule of thumb: Whenever you get back to work on a writing project, go over what you have already written and make it more lucid and fluent. That will improve the writing you have already done and get you ready for what you still have to do. Hemingway did this when he wrote *A Farewell to Arms*: "I was happier than I had ever been. Each day I read the book through to the point where I went on writing and each day I stopped when I was still going good and when I knew what would happen next."[3] Rereading and revising your work will get you back into the work of writing.

4. Get Feedback on Each Draft

It is hard to read our own writing. When we look at what we have written, we tend to see what we meant to say rather than what we actually said. Our words seem clear because we see them from our own perspective and in light of our own understanding.

This is the point of feedback—we need others to tell us what we have written.

Since other people come at our writing from different angles, they can see what is hidden from our point of view. But since they have their own point of view, their vision of our writing is bound to be limited as well: they will see some of it clearly, some in a distorted way, and some aspects not at all. Even the most obtuse and unjust criticism can be inadvertently illuminating and helpful, if it shows how our writing is open to being misread. The hardest task of writing is to look for grains of truth in criticism that seems stupid and unfair. Listen to feedback carefully: pick out the grains of truth, correct the distortions, and ignore the blind spots.

5. Write Until You Can Say the Same Thing in Brief and at Length

You have not fully worked out a path of thought until you can lay it out at different levels of generality: a one-sentence summary, a single paragraph, a few pages, a synopsis of each section, the complete text, and unwritten elaborations on every part of the text. The final aim is to think through the project at many levels of generality and specificity, so that you can see the whole work at different altitudes, zooming in and out from the granular detail visible at ground level to the comprehensive overview available at thirty thousand feet.

The final aim of an academic project, for example, is not just a complete text but a book proposal that includes chapter summaries, a one hundred-word abstract, and a one-sentence distillation of the whole project. The final aim of a screenwriter is not just a complete typescript but may also include a one-minute pitch, a ten-minute pitch, storyboards, reels, and a synopsis of the arc of the story (opening, inciting incident, first act break, midpoint reversal, second act break, and climax). Writing a life story tends to be overwhelming unless we work on telling the story both in brief and at length: a few sentences, a few pages, a few dozen pages, and a few hundred pages.

To think through a text in this way, it helps to write and rewrite different levels of the same project at the same time. Be ready to revise your general view of the whole as you write out specific parts; but also be willing to edit and cut specific parts as your general overview of the project evolves.

6. Proofread Your Penultimate Draft

When you have finished a penultimate draft, ask someone else to proofread it for you. It is easier to proofread the writing of others than our own writing, just as it is easier for us to see the motes in the eyes of others than to see the logs in our own. If you can't find a proofreader, grit your teeth, roll up your sleeves, and go through your writing *one more time*, focusing only on syntax, mechanics, usage, and grammar.

OUTLINE

7. Use the Order of Your Text to Show the Order of Your Subject

The task of composition is not to fit thoughts into a pre-established order, or to let thoughts flow without any order at all. It is to see the intrinsic order of a topic and to structure a text in a way that makes that order visible. Order is neither arbitrary nor given in advance. The work of ordering a text is a work of creative invention. In the words of Milan Kundera, "The composition (the architectural organization of a work) should not be seen as some preexistent matrix, loaned to an author for him to fill up with his invention; the composition itself should be an invention, an invention that engages all the author's originality."[1]

The order of *discovery* moves from the obvious aspects of something to its underlying grounds, as Darwin moved from observable variations in species of birds to the underlying mechanisms of natural selection.

The order of *explanation* moves from underlying grounds to the phenomena they explain, as a scientist might start from the structure of water molecules to explain the six-sided form of snowflakes.

The structure of a text should lay out the structure of the topic itself.

8. Make Outlines

Outlines help to organize thoughts, but different writers use them in different ways.

One way is to start from an outline. Gather your thoughts. List on scratch paper the points you want to make. Then try to figure out how these points fit together. What do readers need to know first? Which points are presupposed by the others and need to be near the start? Which points do readers have to be prepared for and so need to go later in the text? An initial outline is like a blueprint for the text to be written.

Another way is post-outlining. Crank out a rough draft first—a "brain splat" or "vomit draft"—and then distill from it an outline that rearranges the sections into a clear and coherent order.

Some writers take both paths: they start with an initial outline and then revise the outline as they go along.

The final goal is the same: You should be able to summarize the point of each section of your essay and to lay out those points in a way that allows for a clear overview. The outline of your text should articulate the structure of your line of thought.

9. Lay Out Paragraphs in a Coherent Sequence of Steps

The topic sentences of your paragraphs should form a coherent sequence of points. If your topic sentences follow from the previous ones and lead to the next, then your paragraphs will do so too.

10. Start by Indicating the Subject Right Away

The first words should show why a text is worth reading. Get to the point.

Some teachers tell students to start with broad generalizations and then gradually narrow their focus until they reach the specific topic of the essay. This is terrible advice. It is very hard to do well since it is almost impossible to say anything interesting or illuminating at a high level of generality. Start with something specific that gets to the heart of the matter: a story, question, example, quote, statistic, paradox, or claim.

The Handbook of Epictetus starts with his most basic distinction: "Some things are within our power, while others are not."[2]

Rousseau began *The Social Contract* with the paradox he aimed to explain: "Man is born free, and everywhere he is in chains."[3]

Marx started the *Communist Manifesto* with a bold claim: "The history of all society until now is the history of class struggles."[4]

Virginia Woolf began an essay on reading with the question, "How Should One Read a Book?"[5]

Janet Malcolm, in *The Journalist and the Murderer,* laid down the thesis of the whole book in the first sentence: "Every journalist who is not too stupid or too full of himself to notice what is going on knows that what he does is morally indefensible."[6]

Don't futz around. Start by showing right away that at the heart of your topic, there is something compelling that needs to be understood.

ARGUMENT

11. Give Your Readers What They Need to Follow Your Argument

One task of philosophical writing is to start from an average understanding of a topic and to lay out a path by which readers can move step by step toward a genuine understanding. There are two ways to fail in this task.

One way to fail is to assume readers already know everything. The writer adopts the stance of an expert speaking to other experts, who perfectly understand her references, allusions, and technical terminology. The result is *argument by allusion*: a style that does not construct an argument by reading texts, explaining concepts, and laying out a line of thought, but that makes pseudo-arguments by alluding to readings, concepts, and lines of thought that readers are already supposed to know. Good writing is *self-contained* in the sense that it gives readers the tools they need to understand it. This style is good not just for readers, but for writers too, since it takes discipline to translate one's deepest insights into a discourse that is open to everyone.

Another way to fail is to start from an average level of understanding and stay there. The writer adopts the stance of an everyman speaking common sense to regular folks. The assumption is that nothing exceeds the scope of common sense; there is no need to speak anything but plain English, and anyone who writes otherwise is a pretentious phony.

The best writing bridges the gap between average and deeper understanding: it is both sophisticated and down to earth, theoretically informed but free of jargon; simple without being simplistic, able to articulate the deepest insights in plain English without sacrificing rigor, complexity, or precision.

12. Put in Your Text Only What Is Relevant to Your Point

Your basic point can be obscured if you focus too much on subordinate points. Cover subordinate points only at the level of specificity required to make your basic point. Precision does not require an exhaustive treatment of specifics; you can be precise even when you cover a topic quickly and at a high level of generality.

A rule of thumb: When you summarize a story, include in your summary only what your reader needs to know to understand your argument. Everything else is clutter and ought to be cut. It is easy to say things that are correct but unilluminating, just as it is easy to focus on what is interesting but inessential. Writing is a constant struggle not to say what is correct and yet trivial, but to illuminate what is essential.

13. If You Make More Than Two Points, Enumerate Them

Enumeration is an easy way to gather and distinguish a number of related points. However, it should be used with care—it can also be used simply to list points rather than articulate the relations between them. If you enumerate a number of points, lay them out in an order that shows their interrelations.

14. Find the Grains of Truth in Other Views

If someone is in error, it is not enough to dismiss their ideas; you have to find both the grains of truth and the limits of their view. A basic respect for others requires that we show how, if they are wrong, it is not because they are idiots but because their views might *seem* plausible to perfectly reasonable people. Aristotle made this point: "We not only have to say what is true, but also to explain what is false, since this contributes to trust; for when we can say clearly why something appears true when it is not true, this increases trust in the true."[1]

Constructive disagreement takes four steps:

(a) Paraphrase an opposing argument as fairly as possible.

(b) Account for its error by recognizing whatever truth it may contain, laying out the arguments that make it seem reasonable, pointing to the experiences that make it seem plausible, or locating the context within which it makes sense.

(c) Give the reasons you have for your own views. Point out what the opposing argument takes for granted, takes out of context, distorts, confuses, generalizes too far, or simply fails to see.

(d) Lay out your own views as humbly as possible.

15. Do Justice to Views You Think Are Wrong

Don't attack straw men. Don't fight windmills. Be fair to views you oppose. In papers, lay out the strongest version of the arguments against your view, and respond to them as justly as possible. In stories, let the villain make the strongest case against the ethos of the hero, and give the hero every reason to do the wrong thing. Your thinking will be truer if you respond to the strongest version of the views you oppose.

QUESTIONS

16. Use Questions to Introduce Topics

In the *Phaedrus*, Socrates says that "most people are unaware that they do not know what each thing really is."[1] This implies that ignorance is complex—it is not just that we do not know what things are, but that we do not even know that we are ignorant. To start to think, we have to be aware of this twofold ignorance. That is the point of questions. Questions provoke a sense of wonder by pointing to something obscure, something whose obscurity we have not been able to see.

A good question is profoundly illuminating, even if it leaves us with no answers. Milan Kundera made this point with a beautiful image: "A question is like a knife that slices through the stage backdrop and gives us a look at what lies hidden behind it."[2]

One way to introduce a topic is to ask a question about it—a question that helps readers see what is obscure in a topic and what needs to be better grasped and brought to light. Starting with questions invites the reader to think through an argument from the inside, rather than just watch it unfold from the outside. Thinking starts with wonder. Wonder is expressed in questions. Good questions do five things:

a) They point to something *obscure*.

b) They point to what is *not obvious*—to areas of obscurity that are usually hidden by the false clarity of common sense.

c) They get to the heart of the matter—instead of focusing on trivialities, they point to something *essential* that has to be understood in order to understand the matter as a whole.

d) They are not *loaded*—not based on tendentious assumptions. Every question assumes some ideas as given, but good questions rest on carefully considered assumptions, while bad questions thoughtlessly take their assumptions for granted.

e) They point to an issue that is *open*. Bad questions imply a single acceptable answer. Good questions have several plausible answers, about which reasonable people could disagree. (The opposite of an open question is a *leading* question—a question that tacitly leads people to a single, preconceived answer.)

Good questions also tend to be *simple*. The more complicated a question, the more likely it is to be leading, obscure, and confusing. Simpler is better.

17. Prepare Your Readers for Difficult Questions

If the meaning of a question is self-evident, it needs no introduction. "How should one read a book?" is a question that can be asked with no introduction, since it presupposes nothing but common knowledge. A question like this can be the first sentence of a question-based essay.

If a question presupposes ideas unfamiliar to a general audience—if it is framed in technical terms, or if it assumes specialized knowledge, or if it rests on assumptions most readers may not share—then the question has to be introduced before it can be posed.

EXAMPLES

18. Use Regular Examples to Relate the Specific to the General

Some writing is bad because it consists only of abstractions and never bothers to focus on anything particular and concrete. Other writing is bad because it only regurgitates the particular details of experience, without trying to make a general point that might be of interest to anyone other than the writer. A mass of concrete details is as meaningless as a series of empty generalizations. Specifics are meaningful when they illustrate more general phenomena, and generalizations are meaningless unless they can be applied something particular. Use examples to relate the specific and general, the abstract and the concrete.

19. Use Counterexamples to Show the Limits of Common Views

As long as we think only in abstractions, we never have to confront anything that resists our comprehension. The best way to keep our thinking in touch with reality is to start with actual examples as they appear in experience or first-hand testimony. Concrete examples help to show the weaknesses, limits, and blind spots in our thought.

This is the function of *counterexamples*—examples that resist or elude the concepts that are supposed to comprehend them, and so reveal their weaknesses, limitations, or blind spots. Counterexamples are the point of contact between thought and reality—the point of resistance against which we can hone and sharpen our thinking. A high-powered theory without examples is like a muscle car on blocks; it may sound impressive, but it gets us nowhere. Examples are where the rubber meets the road—where abstract thought comes in contact with reality.

20. Choose Examples That Show the Importance of Your Point

Your argument will seem trivial if you illustrate your points with trivial examples. Show why your argument matters by giving examples people actually care about.

QUOTATIONS

21. Do Justice to he Works You Quote

When you quote a passage, take care not to distort, flatten, simplify, or misinterpret the work to which it belongs.

22. Incorporate Quotations in a Grammatically Coherent Way

The grammar of your text should fit the sentences you quote. If you quote a sentence that uses the first person plural, you have to use the first person plural when you introduce the quotation.

23. Don't Put Long Quotations into the Middle of a Sentence

It is better to write a full sentence that leads up to a long quotation.

24. Make Sure the Sense and Context of Quotations Are Clear

Introduce each quotation with a sentence that summarizes what the writer is doing. It usually helps to follow each quotation with a few sentences that explain how you interpret it, but sometimes you can let a quoted passage speak for itself.

25. Put Short Quotations into Quotation Marks

A short quotation is fewer than sixty words, three or fewer lines of prose, or one line of poetry.

26. Set Off Long Quotations in Indented and Single-Spaced Blocks

Use block quotations for anything longer than sixty words, three lines of prose, or one line of poetry. Block quotations do *not* need quotation marks.

PARAGRAPHS

27. Focus Each Paragraph on Just One Topic

A paragraph is a set of sentences that have just one point. Complex points require long paragraphs. Simple points can be made in a one-sentence paragraph. But don't try to cram several points into a single paragraph. If a paragraph contains several distinct points, break it down into several distinct paragraphs.

Try to think in paragraphs—lay out your thoughts in a coherent sequence of points, and make each point in a coherent sequence of sentences. Some teachers fetishize sentences in isolation, as if crafting beautiful sentences were the key to writing well. But the most important unit of writing is not the sentence but the paragraph. Strunk and White were right: "Make the paragraph the unit of composition."[1]

28. Organize Each Paragraph Around a Topic Sentence

Include in each paragraph a sentence that signals its topic. Topic sentences usually summarize the general idea developed in more specific terms in the rest of the paragraph. Most often, they introduce the topic at the start of the paragraph or summarize the point of the paragraph at the end. In general, the clearest topic sentences are the shortest, and short topic sentences (less than one line) are also the most forceful. In the process of writing a text, it sometimes helps to put each topic sentence in *italics*, since this pushes us to be completely clear about the basic point of each paragraph.

29. Place the Key Sentences in a Paragraph at the Start or End

The stress points in a paragraph are the first and last sentences. Whatever you say at the start or end of the paragraph will be taken to be most important. Stress points are the best places to make general points or to pose key questions.

30. Create Continuity Within Paragraphs by Carrying Over Key Words from One Sentence to the Next

By repeating key words from one sentence to another, you can create a network of internal references that hold paragraphs together. Tolstoy did this in *War and Peace*:

> The militiamen brought Prince Andrei to the woods where the carts stood and *the dressing station* was. *The dressing station* consisted of three tents with turned-back flaps pitched at the edge of a *birch grove*. In the *birch grove* stood carts and *horses*. The *horses* were eating oats from their nosebags, and sparrows flew down to them, pecking at the spilled grain.[2]

In this passage, an object in each sentence becomes the subject of the next. The pattern is simple: AB. BC. CD. DE.

Lincoln used a more complex pattern to hold together *The Gettysburg Address*.

> Four score and seven years ago, *our fathers* brought forth on this continent, a new *nation*, conceived in Liberty, and dedicated to the proposition that all men are created equal. Now we are engaged in a great civil *war*, testing whether *that nation*, or any nation so conceived and so dedicated, can long endure. We are met on a great battle*field* of *that war*. We have come to dedicate a portion of *that field*, as a final resting place for those who here gave their lives that *that nation* might live.

In each sentence, Lincoln introduces a new term before repeating a term from the previous sentence with a demonstrative adjective. So the pattern is slightly more complex: AB. CB. DC. DB.

31. Create Continuity Between Paragraphs with Parallel Topic Sentences

If two or three paragraphs are closely related to each other, you can highlight their relation by starting each paragraph with a topic sentence and by giving each topic sentence the same structure.

Maurice Blanchot used parallel topic sentences in the first paragraphs of his beautiful essay, "The Power and the Glory."

> *There was a time when the writer, like the artist, had a relation to glory.* Glorification was his work, and glory was the gift that he gave and received. Glory, in the ancient sense, is the radiance of a presence (sacred or sovereign). To glorify, Rilke says, does not mean to make known; glory is the manifestation of being which comes forth in its magnificence as being, free of what hides it, established in the truth of its revealed presence.
>
> *Glory is followed by renown.* Renown is received more narrowly in the name. The power to name, the force of what denominates, the dangerous assurance of the name (there is danger in being named) becomes the privilege of the man who can name and make what he names understood.
>
> *Renown is followed by reputation,* as truth is by opinion. The fact of publishing—publication—becomes what is essential. This can be taken in a facile sense: the writer is known to the

public, he has a reputation, he seeks to be valued, because he needs value, that is, money. But what arouses the public, which confers value? Publicity. Publicity itself becomes an art, it is the art of all arts, the one that is most important, since it determines the power that determines all the rest.[3]

Note that these paragraphs are held together not just by key words, but by the repetition of the same sentence structure. The first topic sentence introduces the notion of glory. The second relates glory to renown. The third relates renown to reputation. Each paragraph explicates the meaning of its topic in detail, but the details do not obscure the basic flow of thought, because the thoughts are laid out in a sequence of parallel topic sentences.

32. Don't Overuse the Same Paragraph Structure

This gets boring.

33. Keep Verb Tenses Consistent

When you summarize a story or argument, make sure all the verb tenses are consistent.

SENTENCES

34. Be Concise

Every word in a sentence should say something essential. If words can be cut without changing the sense or tone of a sentence, cut them out.

Concise does not mean short; it means no words wasted. The opposite of concise is not *long* but *verbose*. A page-long sentence can be concise if it uses as few words as possible. By contrast, a piece of writing can be verbose, no matter how short it is, if it is bloated with needless words. Gorgias used to boast that, whatever anyone said, he could say the same thing in fewer words: "You will admit that you never heard anyone speak more concisely."[1] This is something to shoot for: Say what you have to say in as few syllables as possible.

35. Use Simple Sentences to Emphasize General Points

Short sentences have more impact than long ones. If you want to emphasize a point, state it as simply as possible.

36. Use Complex Sentences to Articulate Several Related Points

It is best to vary the length of sentences, using short sentences to emphasize basic points and longer sentences to articulate complex points. Writing that has nothing but short sentences feels choppy and monotonous. Long sentences can have a greater richness and harmony than simple declarative sentences. This is why writers use them to heighten the tone of a text, highlight a complex idea, or summarize complicated arguments. A complex sentence can be as clear as a simple one, if each part is clear in itself and if the relations between the parts are clear as well.

Think of Proust. His sentences are very long. And yet, despite the endless qualifications, despite the extended similes that go on forever (like the improvisations of an amateur musician who extends his solos without shame or mercy, knowing that his audience is held hostage by norms of politeness that prevent them from leaving), despite the interminable subordinate clauses which, divided and subdivided in themselves, lead us to constantly anticipate a subject and a verb that they themselves perpetually postpone, so that (like a bored audience desperately anticipating the end of a solo which the soloist's endless noodling constantly postpones) we begin to wonder whether the main clause will ever arrive or whether, perhaps, the preliminary clauses will wander interminably toward a subject that they endlessly defer, if, having read several thousand pages of Proust, we begin to absorb the rhythms of his writing and the counterpoint of his style, we realize that, contrary to our earlier impressions of sentences wandering aimlessly through pages of formless prose, in fact each sentence is as carefully composed as a sonata in which a number of different parts are performed simultaneously by a single instrument, and that just as a master composer can write music in which a single instrument moves back and forth between several melodic lines simultaneously, so that a soloist is able (through the careful modulation of emphasis differentiating successive notes into several parts, and articulating the fragmentary lines of each part into a distinct melody) to create a sense of perfect harmony among many separate and individual voices, each one subordinate to and harmonizing with the main melody, and yet also giving that melody a depth, a rhythm, a resonance that it would not have had on its own, so Proust could write sentences in which the narrative voice is able (through a syntax differentiating the single line of words across the page into a polyphonic counterpoint of ideas, subordinate points, illustrations, and figures of speech) to create a perfectly harmonious sentence, one in which the main line of thought, the melody as it were, remains fluent and intact despite the constant interpolations of subordinate points, and in which these subordinate points give to the main point of the sentence a depth, a rhythm, and a resonance it would not have on its own.

37. Articulate Related Ideas in Similar Sentence Structures

Use parallel sentence structures to indicate a close connection among the ideas they articulate. Parallel construction is especially important in public speaking, since it helps listeners understand the relations between the sentences in a paragraph. This is a key difference between spoken and written discourse. Read the "I Have a Dream" speech by Martin Luther King Jr., and then listen to a recording. What looks repetitious on the page sounds clear and coherent when heard aloud.

38. Don't Overuse the Same Sentence Structure

Use parallel structures when they are appropriate, but don't mechanically repeat the same sentence structure *ad nauseam*.

39. Keep Related Words Together

The meaning of words comes from their relation to one another in a sentence. Don't leave at the end of the sentence a participle that belongs with the verb dangling. Words that belong together in thought should be next to each other in a sentence.

40. Put the Emphatic Words of a Sentence at the End

The end of a sentence is known as *the stress point*. Unless you explicitly emphasize the start or middle of a sentence, whatever you put at the end will be taken as most important. The best way to emphasize the main element in your sentence is to place it at the end.

41. Use Active and Passive Verbs Wherever They Fit Best

Some teachers tell students to avoid the passive voice. This is terrible advice because it puts a formula in place of thought. Instead of following formulas, we need to understand the implications of active and passive verbs and to use them wherever they fit best.

Active verbs highlight activity—the subject of the verb is an agent who acts on others. Passive verbs highlight passivity—the subject of the verb is the passive object of another's action. "Achilles *seized* his sword" has an active verb. "Hector *was seized* by fear" has a verb that is passive. Each kind of verb has its place.

Homer especially was attuned to both our power and our passivity. He used active verbs to highlight the agency of his heroes and passive verbs to highlight their subjection to forces beyond their control. Take this sentence from *The Iliad*: "There the screams and the shouts of triumph rose up together of men *killing* and men *being killed*, and the ground ran with blood."[2] Or this sentence from *The Odyssey*:

> The women surrounded Odysseus and *embraced* him,
> and lovingly kissed his head and shoulders and hands,
> and he *was seized* by a sweet longing to weep and cry.[3]

The women seize Odysseus, and Odysseus is seized by sorrow. Sometimes we act on things, like masters who bend the world to our will, and sometimes we are acted upon, like things in thrall to powers that cannot be mastered.

It is true that active verbs have more force. "I did it" is more forceful than "It was done." With the active verb, I take responsibility for what I have done. Since the passive verb effaces the one responsible for the action, it can be used to evade responsibility, as the Reagan administration used the passive voice to describe wrongdoing in the Iran-Contra scandal: "Mistakes were made."

On the other hand, it sometimes makes sense to use passive verbs. They can be used out of politeness, to avoid shaming someone who has made a mistake. They can be used to shift attention from questions of blame to questions of what to do going forward. They can be used just for the sake of simplicity. Think of the sentence: "The hay has to be brought in before it rains." The passive voice stresses the impersonal necessity of a task. *Who* does the task is less important than *that* it gets done.

The passive voice also fits actions that are so common and thoughtless that they are done by everyone in general rather than anyone in particular. Dostoevsky used the passive voice in *The Brothers Karamazov*, for example, to describe what everyone was saying and doing on the eve of a trial.

> It *was known* that two women rivals were to appear. One of them—that is, Katerina Ivanovna—especially interested everyone; a great many remarkable things *were said* about her, astonishing tales *were told* of her passion for Mitya despite his crime. Special mention *was made* of her pride (she paid visits to almost no one in our town), her "aristocratic connections." It *was said* that she intended to ask the government for permission to

accompany the criminal into penal servitude and to marry him somewhere in the mines, underground. *Awaited* with no less excitement was the appearance in court of Grushenka, Katerina Ivanovna's rival. The meeting before the judges of two rivals—the proud, aristocratic girl, and the "hetaera"—*was awaited* with painful curiosity. . . . In short, there was much talk.[4]

Seven sentences, seven passive verbs. Yes, the passive verbs efface the individuals responsible for the actions, but that effacement is the point. Dostoevsky was not describing individuals who speak in a responsible way; he was describing a common discourse that is irresponsibly repeated by everyone. The whole passage would have been ruined if a pedantic editor had made Dostoevsky change all the passives into active verbs in order to make his writing more "energetic," "vigorous," and "fresh."

There are no rules that can tell us when active or passive verbs will work best. Instead of rules, we need understanding. All the rules in the world are no substitute for intelligence, skill, taste, judgment, knowledge, wit, and wisdom.

42. Avoid Extended Compound Subjects

The subject of a sentence is whatever does the action named by the verb. Compound subjects are formed by making a complex idea, expressed in a number of words, into the subject of a sentence.

The journal *Philosophy and Literature* has an annual Bad Writing Contest, for which readers nominate the worst sentences published each year. In 1998, the winning sentence began with a remarkably long compound subject:

> The move from a structuralist account in which capital is understood to structure social relations in relatively homologous ways to a view of hegemony in which power relations are subject to repetition, convergence, and rearticulation brought the question of temporality into the thinking of structure, and marked a shift from a form of Althusserian theory that takes structural totalities as theoretical objects to one in which the insights into the contingent possibility of structure inaugurate a renewed conception of hegemony as bound up with the contingent sites and strategies of the rearticulation of power.[5]

This sentence is bad not just because it is full of jargon, but because it starts with a compound subject that takes thirty-five words to get to the goddamned verb.

Certain locutions tend to generate extended compound subjects: "The fact that . . ." "The idea that . . . ." These phrases should be used with extreme caution, if at all. It is best to avoid compound subjects altogether.

WORDS

43. Be Precise

A care for thinking requires a care for words. Heidegger wrote that "In the end it is the task of philosophy to protect the *power of the most elementary words* in which human beings express themselves from being flattened by the common understanding to the point where those words can no longer be understood."[1] Sloppy diction shows not just a carelessness with words but a lack of interest in reality. It is a sign not just of lazy thinking, but of an inability to see things for what they are. Arendt made this point in her essay, *On Violence*: "To use [different words] as synonyms not only indicates a certain deafness to linguistic meanings, which would be serious enough, but it also has resulted in a kind of blindness to the realities they correspond to."[2]

44. Use the Simplest Appropriate Word

Why use plain English when there are perfectly good technical terms that no one will understand? Let's just say that if, in the context in which you use them, two words have the same meaning, tone, and connotations, use the simpler one.

45. Use Technical Terms Only If You Know What They Mean

Better to admit our ignorance than to pretend to know what we don't really know. If you use technical terms, you should be able to define them and give clear examples.

46. Introduce Technical Terms in Plain English

If you have to use technical terms when you are writing for a general audience, you need to explain clearly what they mean. One way to do this is to use the term and then explain it. For example, "He had prosopagnosia, an inability to see and recognize faces." Another way is to show how abstract concepts are derived from ordinary language. For example: "Husserl said philosophers should return to things themselves and grasp what they are based on how they show themselves in experience. The study (*logos*) of what shows itself (*phenomena*) he called *phenomenology*."

47. Don't Mix Dead Metaphors

Every abstract concept retains the trace of an old metaphor. The words "concept" and "comprehend," for example, come from metaphors of grasping and holding (the Latin *capere*, "To take, grasp" and *prehendere*, "to seize"). The words "idea" and "insight" come from metaphors of vision (the Greek *eidos*, "aspect, visible form," and the Anglo-Saxon "sight"). Your writing will be more coherent if you use these terms in a way that is consistent with their original sense. It makes more sense to say that an idea is clear or obscure than to say it is easily grasped or incomprehensible, just as it makes more sense to say a concept lets us grasp or comprehend something rather than to see or illuminate it.

48. Use Figurative Language Judiciously

The point of figurative language is not to talk pretty, but to illuminate a topic for which there are no literal terms. A good figure is like a diamond knife—it cuts to the heart of the matter and lays it bare.

49. Avoid Turning Verbs into Nouns

Don't turn verbs into nouns. In other words, don't nominalize verbs. The word "nominalization" is itself a nominalization—it turns an action named by a simple verb into an ugly and opaque abstraction. If you find nominalizations in your writing, turn them back into verbs. Your writing will be cleaner and clearer.

One exception: If you use a verb in one sentence, you may *nominalize* that verb in the next. This kind of *nominalization* ties sentences together and creates a sense of continuity between each sentence and the next.

50. Speak to Others in a Language They Can Understand

Use words that are appropriate to your readers. It is fine to write for experts in the terminology of their field, but we should be able to *translate* our expertise as far as possible into words accessible to a general audience. Technical terms are not "jargon" in themselves; they only become jargon when they are not properly introduced and when they are directed at readers who don't have the background to understand them. If you must use technical words in writing for a general audience, explain them in plain English.

Writing for a general audience is good discipline. Technical terms are a kind of shorthand, so it is easy to string them together without really knowing what they mean. Writing in ordinary language forces us to think through ideas on our own. If you can't lay out your thoughts in plain English, you probably don't really know what you are talking about. Kant made this point in a letter: "Every philosophical work must be susceptible to popularity; if not, it probably conceals nonsense beneath a fog of seeming sophistication."[3] Writing at its best brings together the abstract and the concrete, rarified insight and down-to-earth language, the highest levels of thought and the most common forms of experience. The best writing integrates the highest virtues of theory, knowledge, judgment, and taste with the humbler virtues of craft, skill, hard work, and practical know-how. Some philosophers seem to despise writing that is simple and clear. But simplicity and clarity are not marks of superficiality, but of long, deep, careful thought.

AFTERWORD

I began this book for a course I taught on writing. The basic question of the course was simply: How to write?

As a student, I had taken several courses on writing, and they all taught writing as a craft. Craft was understood as a matter of technical skills, and skills were taught through lists of imperatives that dictated how to construct sentences, organize paragraphs, lay out arguments, and structure stories. But these dictates were detached from any reflection on the practice of writing and its final aims. Writing was reduced to a matter of technique, and the question of how to write was answered in purely technical terms.

This kind of answer seemed incomplete. Yes, writing is a craft. But we can judge the craftsmanship of a work only by understanding the work's purpose, and we can understand a work's purpose only in relation to the ends of human life. A purely technical approach to writing is bound to be incomplete insofar as it ignores questions of purposes and ends. The point of teaching skills is to enable us to write a text, but what is the point of writing a text? For the sake of what? What is the final aim of the practice of writing? Why write?

This question has several common answers. One answer has to do with truth—the point of writing is to communicate knowledge for the sake of general enlightenment. Another answer has to do with goodness—the point of writing is to effect some sort of good, whether higher goods such as freedom and justice or lower goods such as victory, fame, and enormous piles of money. A third answer has to do with beauty—the point of writing is to create works whose aesthetic beauty can be enjoyed as an end in itself.

These answers show the limits of teaching writing as a set of skills. Skills are always part of some practice; every practice exists for the sake of some end; practices are ultimately guided by some vision of the ends of human life. The question of how to write can never be purely technical. Questions of writing are always implicated in questions of philosophy. The question of how to write is rooted in the question of how to live.

So when I began to teach my own Composition course, twenty-five years ago, I focused on the philosophy of writing. The course was based on the notion that technical questions are implicated in deeper questions of truth, goodness, and beauty. To work through these questions, I began to write out my thoughts, and it was this tentative writing that led me to start this book.

At the start, I took for granted the modern division of philosophy into epistemology, moral philosophy, and aesthetics. I assumed the essential traits of writing could be understood in terms of the basic concepts of these fields: the truth of writing could be understood in terms of epistemology; the goodness of writing in terms of moral philosophy; and the beauty of writing in terms of aesthetics.

This assumption was not entirely wrong. The basic concepts of these fields are perfectly adequate for most kinds of writing. Questions of epistemology are framed in terms that are adequate to any writing that aims to communicate knowledge. Questions of moral philosophy are framed in terms that are adequate to any writing that aims to do what is right. Questions of aesthetics are framed in terms that are adequate to any writing that aims at free beauty.

But the more I tried to understand writing in terms of these fields of philosophy, the less adequate their basic concepts appeared. This was especially true of the authors I loved most—authors for whom writing was not just a tool of communication, or a medium of self-expression, or an imitation of living speech, but a daily discipline and a path to understanding. The more carefully I tried to apply modern concepts to their texts, the more clearly it appeared that these concepts failed to comprehend what I loved most in their work. As long as I thought in these terms, I could not grasp what was essential.

Writing this book changed the terms in which I think. I came to think that, at its best, the truth of writing cannot be understood in epistemological terms; the goodness of writing exceeds the sphere of moral philosophy; and the beauty of writing eludes the basic concepts of aesthetics. To truly understand the practice of writing, we have to rethink modern concepts of truth, goodness, and beauty.

This rethinking is a labor of love. It is love of truth that moves us to rethink common concepts of truth; love of goodness that attunes us to the limits of moral concepts of the good; love of beauty that draws us to recognize a kind of beauty that in aesthetic terms is simply inconceivable.

In working on this book, over the course of twenty-five years, I came to see that the question of writing, which seems shallow and marginal, actually leads to the deepest and most central questions of philosophy.

The writing I love most aims at a kind of understanding that exceeds the domains of epistemology, moral philosophy, and aesthetics. Its authors do not try to communicate knowledge, or do what is right, or create free beauty. Instead, they try to reach and articulate a true understanding of the highest goods of human life. The traditional word for this kind of understanding is "wisdom." This writing eludes the grasp of modern philosophical concepts because it aims at wisdom.

This line of thought led to a conclusion that was completely unexpected. Philosophy used to be a search for wisdom. Wisdom was the aim of a philosophical life. But if philosophy is the love of wisdom, and if wisdom eludes the basic concepts of modern thought, then modern thought cannot grasp the aim of philosophy. We not only have to rethink our views of writing. We also have to rethink our views of philosophy itself.

Today if you ask philosophers for wisdom, most will look at you with condescension and pity. For them, philosophy is either a field of science or a kind of theory or an art of living. But wisdom (*sophia*) is neither science (*episteme*), nor theory (*theoria*), nor art (*techne*). If most philosophers today are silent on the question of wisdom, it is because wisdom lies beyond the limits of their discourse. They do not speak of wisdom because it eludes the basic concepts of modern thought: the truth of wisdom exceeds the scope of epistemology; the goodness of wisdom transcends moral goodness; and the beauty of wisdom is beyond the field of aesthetics. If we follow the question of writing into the depths, we are led to rethink the meaning of truth, goodness, and beauty. And this rethinking does not leave philosophy unchanged. It pushes us not just to rethink the nature of writing, but also to rethink the nature of philosophy itself. The question of writing eventually leads to the question: What is philosophy?

For many thinkers today, the question of philosophy is closed. They are sure they already know what it is. But the question of writing may again open up the question of philosophy. And the art of writing may again be practiced as a way to search for wisdom.

June 30, 2025

WORKS CITED

Aeschylus. *Oresteia*. Edited and translated by Alan H. Sommerstein. Cambridge, MA: Harvard University Press, 2008.

Agamben, Giorgio. *The Man Without Content*. Translated by Georgia Albert. Stanford, CA: Stanford University Press, 1999.

Anzaldúa, Gloria. "Speaking in Tongues: A Letter to Third World Women Writers." In *Words in Our Pockets*. Edited by Celeste West. Paradise, CA: Dustbooks, 1985.

Aquinas, Thomas. *Truth, Volume I, Questions I-IX*. Translated by Robert W. Mulligan, S. J. Eugene, OR: Wipf and Stock Publishers, 2008.

Arendt, Hannah. *Between Past and Future*. New York: Penguin Books, 1993.

Arendt, Hannah. *Essays in Understanding*. Edited by Jerome Kohn. New York: Harcourt Brace & Company, 1994.

Arendt, Hannah. *The Human Condition*. Chicago, IL: University of Chicago Press, 1989.

Arendt, Hannah. *Lectures on Kant's Political Philosophy*. Edited by Ronald Beiner. Chicago, IL: University of Chicago Press, 1989.

Arendt, Hannah. *Men in Dark Times*. New York: Harcourt Brace & Company, 1995.

Arendt, Hannah. *On Violence*. New York: Harcourt Brace & Company, 1970.

Aristotle. *Athenian Constitution, Eudemian Ethics, Virtues and Vices*. Translated by H. Rackham. Cambridge, MA: Harvard University Press, 1971.

Aristotle. *Nicomachean Ethics*. Translated by H. Rackham. Cambridge, MA: Harvard University Press, 1994.

Arndt, Michael. www.pandemoniuminc.com.

Augustine. *Against the Epistle of Manichaeus, Called Fundamental*. Translated by Richard Stothert. Savage, MN: Lighthouse Publishing, 2017.

Augustine. *Confessions*. Translated by Henry Chadwick. New York: Oxford University Press, 1991.

Aurelius, Marcus. *The Emperor's Handbook*. Translated by Scot and David Hicks. New York: Scribner, 2002.

Aurelius, Marcus. *Marcus Aurelius*. Translated by C. R. Haines. Cambridge, MA: Harvard University Press, 1930.

Baumgarten, Alexander. *Reflections on Poetry*. Translated by Karl Aschenbrenner and William B. Holther. Berkeley: University of California Press, 1954.

Blanchot, Maurice. *The Book to Come*. Translated by Charlotte Mandell. Stanford, CA: Stanford University Press, 2003.

Blanchot, Maurice. *La Part de Feu*. Paris: Gallimard, 1949.

Blanchot, Maurice. *Le livre à venir*. Paris: Éditions Gallimard, 1959.

Blanchot, Maurice. *The Work of Fire*. Translated by Charlotte Mandell. Stanford, CA: Stanford University Press, 1995.

Bourdieu, Pierre. *Distinction*. Translated by Richard Nice. New York: Routledge, 2010.

Brooks, Paul. *House of Life: Rachel Carson at Work*. New York: Houghton Mifflin Harcourt, 1993.

Carpenter, Anne. *Theo-Poetics*. Notre Dame, IN: Notre Dame University Press, 2015.

Darwin, Charles. *The Origin of Species*. Edited by Gillian Beer. New York: Oxford University Press, 1996.

De Beauvoir, Simone. *The Second Sex*. Translated by H. M. Parshley. New York: Knopf, 1993.

Descartes, René. *Discourse on Method and Meditations on First Philosophy*, 4th ed. Translated by Donald A. Cress. Indianapolis: Hackett, 1998.

Dostoyevsky, Fyodor. *The Brothers Karamazov*. Translated by Richard Pevear and Larissa Volokhonsky. New York: Knopf, 1992.

Douglas, J. D., ed. *The New Greek-English Interlinear New Testament,* The Revised Standard Version. Translated by Robert K. Brown and Philip W. Comfort. Wheaton, IL: Tyndale Publishers, 1990.

Dreyfus, Hubert. *Skillful Coping*. New York: Oxford University Press, 2016.

Dreyfus, Hubert and Charles Taylor. *Retrieving Realism*. Cambridge, MA: Harvard University Press, 2015.

Epictetus. *Discourses, Books 1-2*. Translated by W. A. Oldfather. Cambridge, MA: Harvard University Press, 1925.

Epictetus. *Discourses, Fragments, Handbook*. Translated by Robin Hard. New York: Oxford University Press, 2014.

Foucault, Michel. *The Hermeneutics of the Subject.* Edited by Frédéric Gros. Translated by Graham Burchell. New York: Palgrave Macmillan, 2005.

Foucault, Michel. *Remarks on Marx.* Translated by R. James Goldstein and James Cascaito. New York: Semiotext(e), 1991.

Foucault, Michel. "Writing the Self" in *Foucault and His Interlocutors.* Edited by Arnold I. Davidson. Chicago, IL: University of Chicago Press, 1997.

Gadamer, Hans-Georg. *Truth and Method.* Translated by Joel Weinsheimer and Donald G. Marshall. New York: Continuum, 1993.

Ganz, Marshall. "Telling Your Public Story: Self, Us, Now." https://www.scribd.com/document/551088014/Public-Story-Worksheet07Ganz.

Girard, René. *Job the Victim of his People.* Translated by Yvonne Freccero. Stanford, CA: Stanford University Press, 1987.

Hadot, Pierre. *The Inner Citadel.* Translated by Michael Chase. Cambridge, MA: Harvard University Press, 2001.

Harries, Karsten. *The Ethical Function of Architecture.* Cambridge, MA: MIT Press, 1998.

Hauerwas, Stanley. *Hannah's Child: A Theologian's Memoir.* Grand Rapids, MI: William B. Eerdmans Publishing, 2010.

Hegel, Georg Wilhelm Friedrich. *Aesthetics: Lectures on Fine Art, Volume One.* Translated by T. M. Knox. New York: Oxford University Press, 1999.

Heidegger, Martin. *Basic Problems of Phenomenology.* Translated by Albert Hofstadter. Bloomington: Indiana University Press, 1988.

Heidegger, Martin. *Being and Time.* Translated by Joan Stambaugh. Revised by Dennis J. Schmidt. Albany, NY: SUNY Press, 2010.

Heidegger, Martin. *The Essence of Truth.* Translated by Ted Sadler. New York: Continuum, 2002.

Heidegger, Martin. *Introduction to Metaphysics.* Translated by Gregory Fried and Richard Polt. New Haven, CT: Yale University Press, 2000.

Heidegger, Martin. *Nietzsche, Volume I: The Will to Power as Art.* Translated by David Farrell Krell. New York: Harper & Row, 1979.

Heidegger, Martin. *Off the Beaten Track.* Edited and Translated by Julian Young and Kenneth Haynes. New York: Cambridge University Press, 2002.

Heidegger, Martin. *Pathmarks*. Edited by William McNeill. New York: Cambridge University Press, 1998.

Heidegger, Martin. *Sein und Zeit*. Tübingen. Max Niemeyer Verlag, 1986.

Hemingway, Ernest. *A Farewell to Arms*. New York: Scribner, 1957.

Hesiod. *Theogony, Works and Days, Testimonia*. Translated by Glenn W. Most. Cambridge, MA: Harvard University Press, 2006.

Homer. *The Iliad*. Translated by Richmond Lattimore. Chicago, IL: University of Chicago Press, 1961.

Homer. *Iliadis XIII-XXIV*. Edited by David B. Monro and Thomas W. Allen. New York: Oxford University Press, 1988.

Homer. *The Odyssey*. Translated by Robert Fagles. New York: Penguin, 1996.

Homer. *The Odyssey*. Translated by Emily Wilson. New York: Norton, 2018.

Homer. *The Odyssey: Books 1-12*. Translated by A. T. Murray. Revised by George Dimock. Cambridge, MA: Harvard University Press, 1995.

Homer. *The Odyssey: Books 13-24*. Translated by A. T. Murray. Revised by George Dimock. Cambridge, MA: Harvard University Press, 1995.

Hugh of St. Victor. *The Didascalion*. Translated by Jerome Taylor. New York: Columbia University Press, 1991.

Jaspers, Karl. *Plato and Augustine*. Translated by Ralph Manheim. New York: Harcourt Brace & Company, 1962.

Joyce, James. *Portrait of the Artist as a Young Man*. Ware: Wordsworth Editions, 2001.

Kant, Immanuel. *An Answer to the Question: "What Is Enlightenment?"*. Translated by H. B. Nisbet. New York: Penguin Books, 2009.

Kant, Immanuel. *Critique of Judgment*. Translated by J. H. Bernard. New York: Hafner Press, 1951.

Kaufmann, Walter. *Tragedy and Philosophy*. Princeton, NJ: Princeton University Press, 1968.

Kundera, Milan. *The Art of the Novel*. Translated by Linda Asher. New York: Harper & Row, 1993.

Kundera, Milan. *Testaments Betrayed*. Translated by Linda Asher. New York: HarperPerennial, 1995.

Kundera, Milan. *The Unbearable Lightness of Being*. Translated by Michael Henry Heim. New York: Harper & Row, 1987

Laertius, Diogenes. *Lives of Eminent Philosophers, Volume I*. Translated by R. D. Hicks. Cambridge, MA: Harvard University Press, 2006.

Laertius, Diogenes. *Lives of Eminent Philosophers, Volume II*. Translated by R. D. Hicks. Cambridge, MA: Harvard University Press, 1931.

Liddell, Henry G., Robert Scott, and Henry S. Jones. *Greek-English Lexicon*, Abridged ed. London: Oxford University Press, 1989.

MacIntyre, Alasdair. *After Virtue*, 3rd ed. Notre Dame, IN. University of Notre Dame Press, 2015.

Malcolm, Janet. *The Journalist and the Murderer*. New York: Vintage Press, 1990.

Marion, Jean-Luc. *Givenness & Revelation*. Translated by Stephen E. Lewis. New York: Oxford University Press, 2016.

Marx, Karl. *The Communist Manifesto*. New York: Verso, 1998.

Morrison, Toni. "I Know How to Write Forever." *The New York Times*, August 6, 2019.

Murdoch, Iris. *Acastos*. New York: Viking, 1987.

Nalbantian, Suzanne and Paul M. Matthes, eds. *Secrets of Creativity: What Neuroscience, the Arts, and Our Minds Reveal*. New York: Oxford University Press, 2020.

Nietzsche, Friedrich. *Also Sprach Zarathustra*. Munich: GoldmannVerlag, 1989.

Nietzsche, Friedrich. *Beyond Good and Evil*. Translated by Judith Norman. New York: Cambridge University Press, 2010.

Nietzsche, Friedrich. *Ecce Homo*. Translated by R. J. Hollingdale. New York: Penguin Books, 1992.

Nietzsche, Friedrich. *Ecce Homo: Wie Man Wird, Was Man Ist*. Las Vegas, NV: Anonymous, 2024.

Nietzsche, Friedrich. *The Gay Science*. Edited by Bernard Williams. Translated by Josefine Nauckhoff. New York: Cambridge University Press, 2006.

Nietzsche, Friedrich. *Human, All Too Human*. Translated by R. J. Hollingdale. New York: Cambridge University Press, 1996.

Nietzsche, Friedrich. *On the Genealogy of Morals*. Translated by Carol Diethe. Edited by Keith Ansell-Pearson. New York: Cambridge University Press, 2002.

Nietzsche, Friedrich. *Thus Spoke Zarathustra*. Translated by R. J. Hollingdale. New York: Penguin, 1969.

Nietzsche, Friedrich. *Zur Genealogie der Moral*. Frankfurt: Insel Verlag, 1991.
Pieper, Josef. *Enthusiasm & Divine Madness: On the Platonic Dialogue Phaedrus*. South Bend, IN: St. Augustine Press, 2000.
Pieper, Josef. *Living the Truth*. Translated by Lothar Krauth. San Francisco: Ignatius Press, 1989.
Plato. *Euthyphro, Apology, Crito, Phaedo, Phaedrus*. Translated by Harold North Fowler. Cambridge, MA: Harvard University Press, 2005.
Plato. *Lysis, Symposium, Gorgias*. Translated by W. R. M. Lamb. Cambridge, MA: Harvard University Press, 1991.
Plotinus. *The Enneads*. Translated by Stephen MacKenna. New York: Penguin, 1991.
Proust, Marcel. *À l'ombre des jeunes filles en fleurs*. Paris: Gallimard, 1988.
Proust, Marcel. *Du Côté de Chez Swann*. Paris: Gallimard, 1988.
Proust, Marcel. *Le Temps retrouvé*. Paris: Gallimard, 1990.
Proust, Marcel. *Swann's Way*. Translated by C. K. Scott Moncrieff and Terence Kilmartin. Revised by D. J. Enright. New York: Modern Library, 1992.
Proust, Marcel. *Time Regained*. Translated by C. K. Scott Moncrieff and Terence Kilmartin. Revised by D. J. Enright. New York: Modern Library, 1992.
Proust, Marcel. *Within a Budding Grove*. Translated by C. K. Scott Moncrieff and Terence Kilmartin. Revised by D. J. Enright. New York: Modern Library, 1992.
Ricoeur, Paul. *Hermeneutics & the Human Sciences*. Translated by John B. Thompson. New York: Cambridge University Press, 1994.
Ricoeur, Paul. *Oneself As Another*. Translated by Kathleen Blamey. Chicago: University of Chicago Press, 1992.
Rilke, Rainer Maria. *Briefe an einen jungen Dichter*. Leipzig: Insel Verlag, 1929.
Rilke, Rainer Maria. *Letters to a Young Poet*. Translated by Stephen Mitchell. New York: Modern Library, 2001.
Rousseau, Jean-Jacques. *The Social Contract*. Translated by Judith Masters. New York: St. Martin's Press, 1978.
Rufus, Musonius. *Stoic Fragments*. Translated by Cora Lutz. New Delhi: Isha Books, 2013.

Saunders, George. *A Swim in a Pond in the Rain*. New York: Random House, 2021.

Scheler, Max. *Ressentiment*. Translated by Lewis B. Coser and William W. Holdheim. Milkwaukee, WI: Marquette University Press, 1998.

Seneca. *Letters on Ethics*. Translated by Margaret Graver and A. A. Long. Chicago, IL: University of Chicago Press, 2015.

Shelley, Percy Bysshe. *Shelley's Poetry and Prose*. Edited by Donald H. Reiman and Neil Freistat. New York: Norton, 2002.

Stendhal. *The Life of Henry Brulard*. Translated by John Surrock. New York: The New York Review of Books, 2002.

Strunk, William and E. B. White. *Elements of Style,* 4th ed. New York: Longman, 1999.

Taylor, Charles. *The Language Animal*. Cambridge, MA: Harvard University Press, 2016.

Taylor, Charles. *Philosophical Arguments*. Cambridge, MA: Harvard University Press, 1997.

Taylor, Charles. *Sources of the Self*. Cambridge, MA: Harvard University Press, 1989.

Tchaikovsky, Modeste. *The Life and Letters of Pyotr Ilyich Tchaikovsky*, Edited by Rosa Newmarch. New York: John Lane Company, 1906.

Thoreau, Henry David. *Walden and Resistance to Civil Government*. Edited by William Rossi. New York: Norton, 1992.

Tolstoy, Leo. *A Confession and Other Religious Writings*. New York: Penguin, 1987.

Tolstoy, Leo. *The Death of Ivan Ilyich*. Translated by Lynn Solotaroff. New York: Bantam Classics, 2004.

Tolstoy, Leo. *War and Peace*. Translated by Richard Pevear and Larissa Volokhonsky. New York: Vintage Books, 2008.

Tracy, David. *Plurality and Ambiguity*. San Francisco: Harper & Row, 1987.

Trimble, John. *Writing With Style*. New York: Prentice Hall, 2011.

Vendler, Helen. *Poems, Poets, Poetry,* Third Edition. New York: Bedford Press, 2010.

Wermuth, Paul Charles. *Modern Essays on Writing and Style*. New York: Holt, Rinehart, Winston, 1969.

Williams, Bernard. *Ethics and the Limits of Philosophy.* Cambridge, MA: Harvard University Press, 1985.

Woolf, Virginia. *How Should One Read a Book?* London: Laurence King, 2020.

Zinsser, William. *On Writing Well,* 5th ed. New York: Harper & Row, 1976.

NOTES

Why Write?

1 Toni Morrison, "I Know How to Write Forever," *The New York Times*, August 6, 2019.

2 Epictetus, *Discourses, Fragments, Handbook*, trans. Robin Hard (New York: Oxford University Press, 2014), 73 (2.1.32) (translation modified).

3 Friedrich Nietzsche, *Human, All Too Human*, trans. R. J. Hollingdale (New York: Cambridge University Press, 1996), 332 and 342.

4 Hannah Arendt, *Essays in Understanding*, ed. Jerome Kohn (New York: Harcourt Brace & Company, 1994), 3.

5 Michel Foucault, *Remarks on Marx*, trans. R. James Goldstein and James Cascaito (New York: Semiotext(e), 1991), 27.

6 Gloria Anzaldúa, "Speaking in Tongues: A Letter to Third World Women Writers," in *Words in Our Pockets*, ed. Celeste West (Paradise, CA: Dustbooks, 1985), 222–3.

Language

1 See Charles Taylor, *The Language Animal* (Cambridge, MA: Harvard University Press, 2016).

2 The distinction between genuine and authentic understanding comes from section 31 of *Being and Time*. See Martin Heidegger, *Being and*

Time, trans. Joan Stambaugh, revised by Dennis Schmidt (Albany, NY: SUNY Press, 2010), 141.

3 William Zinsser, *On Writing Well,* Fifth Edition (New York: Harper Collins, 1976), vii.

4 Walter Kaufmann, *Tragedy and Philosophy* (Princeton, NJ: Princeton University Press, 1968), xvii.

5 Stanley Hauerwas, *Hannah's Child: A Theologian's Memoir* (Grand Rapids, MI: William B. Eerdmans Publishing Company, 2010), 235.

Thinking

1 Martin Heidegger, *Pathmarks,* ed. William McNeill (New York: Cambridge University Press, 1998), 275.

2 On scientific misconceptions of thinking, see Hubert Dreyfus and Charles Taylor, *Retrieving Realism* (Cambridge, MA: Harvard University Press, 2015), 1–26.

Truth

1 Charles Taylor, *Philosophical Arguments* (Cambridge, MA: Harvard University Press, 1997), 12.

2 Paul Ricoeur, *Hermeneutics & the Human Sciences,* trans. John B. Thompson (New York: Cambridge University Press, 1994), 53.

3 Jean-Luc Marion, *Givenness and Revelation,* trans. Stephen E. Lewis (New York: Oxford University Press, 2016), 20.

4 *"Veritas est qua ostenditur id quod est."* Augustine, *De vera religione*, ch. 36. Quoted in Josef Pieper, *Living the Truth*, trans. Lothar Krauth (San Francisco: Ignatius Press, 1989), 61.

5 Thomas Aquinas, *Truth, Volume I, Questions I-IX*, trans. Robert W. Mulligan, S. J. (Eugene, Oregon: Wipf and Stock Publishers, 2008).

6 James Joyce, *Portrait of the Artist as a Young Man* (Ware: Wordsworth Editions, 2001), xvi.

7 David Tracy, *Plurality and Ambiguity* (San Francisco: Harper & Row, 1987), 28–9.

8 Martin Heidegger, *The Essence of Truth*, trans. Ted Sadler (New York: Continuum Press, 2002), 7.

9 Homer, *The Odyssey: Books 1-12*, trans. A. T. Murray, rev. George Dimock (Cambridge, MA: Harvard University Press, 1995), 54–5 (Book II, line 106). The original is: ὣς τρίετες μὲν ἔληθε δόλῳ καὶ ἔπειθεν Ἀχαιούς.

10 Homer, *The Odyssey: Books 13-24*, trans. A. T. Murray, rev. George Dimock (Cambridge, MA: Harvard University Press, 1995), 14–17 (Book 13, lines 187–194). "Therefore, all things seemed strange to their ruler" translates "τοὔνεκ᾽ ἄρ᾽ ἀλλοειδέα φαινέσκετο πάντα ἄνακτι."

11 Homer, *The Odyssey: Books 13-24*, 26–7 (Book 13, lines 344–352). "So spoke the goddess, and scattered the mist, and the land appeared" is a translation of "ὣς εἰποῦσα θεὰ σκέδασ᾽ ἠέρα, εἴσατο δὲ χθών."

12 Marcel Proust, *Swann's Way*, trans. C. K. Scott Moncrieff and Terence Kilmartin, rev. D. J. Enright (New York: Modern Library, 1992), 131–132. Marcel Proust, *Du côté de chez Swann* (Paris: Gallimard, 1988), 94.

13 Rainer Maria Rilke, *Letters to a Young Poet*, trans. Stephen Mitchell (New York: Modern Library, 2001), 23–4. Rainer Maria Rilke, *Briefe an einen jungen Dichter* (Leipzig: Insel Verlag, 1929), 17.

14 Marcel Proust, *Time Regained*, trans. C. K. Scott Moncrieff and Terence Kilmartin, rev. D. J. Enright (New York: Modern Library, 1993), 299. Marcel Proust, *Le Temps retrouvé* (Paris: Gallimard, 1990), 202.

Goodness

1 Friedrich Nietzsche, *The Gay Science*, ed. Bernard Williams, trans. Josefine Nauckhoff (New York: Cambridge University Press, 2006), 182.

2 Aristotle lays out this view in *The Nicomachean Ethics* 1102b.

3 Paul Ricoeur, *Oneself as Another*, trans. Kathleen Blamey (Chicago, IL: University of Chicago Press, 1992), 203.

4 Charles Taylor, *Sources of the Self* (Cambridge, MA: Harvard University Press, 1989), 64.

5 Bernard Williams, *Ethics and the Limits of Philosophy* (Cambridge, MA: Harvard University Press, 1985), 6

6 Heidegger, *Being and Time*, 156–7.

7 John Trimble, *Writing With Style* (New York: Prentice Hall, 2011), 3.

8 https://www.brainpickings.org/2018/01/18/t-s-eliot-alice-quinn-letter/.

9 Rachel Carson, quoted in Paul Brooks, *House of Life: Rachel Carson at Work* (New York: Houghton Mifflin Harcourt, 1993), 3.

10 Rilke, *Letters to a Young Poet*, 6–8 and 8–9. Rilke, *Briefe an einen jungen Dichter*, 8 and 9.

11 Maurice Blanchot, *The Work of Fire*, trans. Charlotte Mandell (Stanford, CA: Stanford University Press, 1995), 307. Maurice Blanchot, *La Part de Feu* (Paris: Gallimard, 1949), 299.

12 Marcel Proust, *Within a Budding Grove*, trans. C. K. Scott Moncrieff and Terence Kilmartin, rev. D. J. Enright (New York: Modern Library, 1992), 210. Marcel Proust, *À l'ombre des jeunes filles en fleurs* (Paris: Gallimard, 1988), 149.

13 Proust, *Time Regained*, 302 (translation modified). Proust, *Le Temps Retrouvé*, 204.

Beauty

1 Plotinus, *The Enneads*, trans. Stephen MacKenna (New York: Penguin, 1991), 47.

2 Georg Wilhelm Friedrich Hegel, *Aesthetics: Lecture on Fine Art*, Vol. 1, trans. T. M. Knox (New York: Oxford University Press, 1999), 103.

3 Alexander Baumgarten, *Reflections on Poetry*, trans. Karl Aschenbrenner and William B. Holther (Berkeley: University of California Press, 1954), 78.

4 The distinction between "free" and "dependent" beauty was laid out by Kant in section 16 of the Third Critique. Immanuel Kant, *The Critique of Judgment*, trans. J. H. Bernard (New York: Hafner Press, 1951), 65–8.

5 "The pleasure of learning and recognizing new and old patterns is probably the source of our deepest pleasure in art." Helen Vendler, *Poems, Poets, Poetry, Third Edition* (New York: Bedford, 2010), 77.

6 "Form, in the medieval sense, encapsulates what makes up the beautiful: proportion, integrity, and *claritas*." Anne Carpenter, *Theo-Poetics* (Notre Dame, IN: University of Notre Dame Press, 2015), 53.

7 Pierre Bourdieu, *Distinction*, trans, Richard Nice (New York: Routledge, 2010).

8 Martin Heidegger, *Introduction to Metaphysics*, trans. Gregory Fried and Richard Polt (New Haven, CT: Yale University Press, 2000), 140.

9 Hans-Georg Gadamer, *Truth and Method*, trans. Joel Weinsheimer and Donald G. Marshall (New York: Continuum Books, 1993), 116.

10 Giorgio Agamben, *The Man Without Content*, trans. Georgia Albert (Stanford, CA: Stanford University Press, 1999), 2 and 6.

11 Karsten Harries, *The Ethical Function of Architecture* (Cambridge, MA: MIT Press, 1998), xii.

12 Aristotle, *Athenian Constitution, Eudemian Ethics, Virtues and Vices*, trans. H. Rackham (Cambridge, MA: Harvard University Press, 1971), 472–3 (1248b36-37). The original is: καλὰ δ'ἐστὶν αἵ τε ἀρεταὶ καὶ τὰ ἔργα τὰ ἀπὸ τῆς ἀρετῆς.

13 This list of virtues is taken from Book Six of Aristotle, *Nicomachean Ethics*, trans. H. Rackham (Cambridge, MA: Harvard University Press, 1994).

14 Plato, *Lysis, Symposium, Gorgias*, trans. W. R. M. Lamb (Cambridge, MA: Harvard University Press, 1991), 48–9 [216D]. Plato's words are: Λέγω γὰρ τἀγαθὸν καλὸν εἶναι.

15 Marcus Aurelius, *Marcus Aurelius*, trans. C. R. Haines (Cambridge, MA: Harvard University Press, 1930), 26–7. Translation modified. Marcus' actual words are: ἐγὼ δὲ τεθεωρηκὼς τὴν φύσιν τοῦ ἀγαθοῦ, ὅτι καλόν, καὶ τοῦ κακοῦ, ὅτι αἰσχρόν.

16 Nietzsche, quoted in Martin Heidegger, *Nietzsche, Volume I: The Will to Power as Art*, trans. David Farrell Krell (New York: Harper & Row, 1979), 111.

17 *Kalos* and *aischros* are used in this sense in lines 436–440 of Book Twenty One. See *The Iliad*, trans. Richmond Lattimore (Chicago, IL: University of Chicago Press, 1961), 430. Homer, *Iliadis XIII-XXIV*, ed. David B. Monro and Thomas W. Allen (New York: Oxford University Press, 1988), 202.

18 John 10:11. *New Greek-English Interlinear New Testament*, The Revised Standard Version, ed. J. D. Douglas, trans. Robert K. Brown and

Philip W. Comfort (Wheaton, IL: Tyndale Publishers, 1990), 361. The original is: ἐγώ εἰμι ὁ ποιμὴν ὁ καλός. ὁ ποιμὴν ὁ καλὸς τὴν ψυχὴν αὐτοῦ τίθησιν ὑπὲρ τῶν προβάτων.

19 Henry David Thoreau, *Walden and Resistance to Civil Government*, ed. William Rossi (New York: Norton, 1992), 61.

20 Max Scheler, *Ressentiment*, trans. Lewis B. Coser and William W. Holdheim (Milwaukee, WI: Marquette University Press, 1998), 54–5.

21 Friedrich Nietzsche, *On the Genealogy of Morality*, ed. Keith Ansell-Pearson, trans. Carol Diethe (New York: Cambridge University Press, 2002), 46 (translation modified).

22 Plato, *Euthyphro, Apology, Crito, Phaedo, Phaedrus*, 512–13 (259e5-7). Translation modified. The original is: Τίς οὖν ὁ τρόπος τοῦ καλῶς τε καὶ μὴ γράφειν;

23 Plato, *Euthyphro, Apology, Crito, Phaedo, Phaedrus*, 516–17 (260e5-7) (translation modified).

Inspiration

1 Plato, *Euthyphro, Apology, Crito, Phaedo, Phaedrus*, 468–9 (245a1-9) (translation modified).

2 My reading of Plato is indebted to Josef Pieper, *Enthusiasm & Divine Madness: On the Platonic Dialogue Phaedrus* (South Bend, IN: St. Augustine Press, 2000).

3 Hesiod, *Theogony, Works and Days, Testimonia*, trans. Glenn W. Most (Cambridge, MA: Harvard University Press, 2006), 4–5. The original is: ἐνέπνευσαν δε μοι αὐδὴν θέσπιν.

4 Homer, *The Odyssey*, trans. Robert Fagles (New York: Penguin, 1996), 450.

5 Percy Bysshe Shelley, "A Defense of Poetry," in *Shelley's Poetry and Prose*, ed. Donald H. Reiman and Neil Fraistat (New York: Norton, 2002), 532.

6 Dmitri Mendeleev, quoted in *Secrets of Creativity: What Neuroscience, the Arts, and Our Minds Reveal*, ed. Suzanne Nalbantian and Paul M. Matthews (New York: Oxford University Press, 2020), 136.

7 Friedrich Nietzsche, *Ecce Homo*, trans. R. J. Hollingdale (New York: Penguin Books, 1992), 72–3. Nietzsche, *Ecce Homo: Wie Man Wird, Was Man Ist*, 52–3.

8 "*Der Begriff Offenbarung . . . beschreibt einfach den Thatbestand.*"

9 "*Plötzlich, mit unsäglicher Sicherheit und Feinheit, Etwas sichtbar, hörbar wird . . . . wie ein Blitz leuchtet ein Gedanke auf . . . .*"

10 "*Man hört, man sucht nicht; man nimmt, man fragt nicht, wer da giebt . . . .*"

11 Nietzsche, *Ecce Homo*, 73. Nietzsche, *Ecce Homo: Wie Man Wird, Was Man Ist*, 53.

12 "*Alles geschieht im höchsten Grade unfreiwillig, aber wie in einem Sturme von Freiheits-Gefühl, von Unbedingtsein, von Macht, von Göttlichkeit.*"

13 Here I am indebted to Hans-Georg Gadamer: "To understand a foreign language means that we do not need to translate it into our own. When we really master a language, then no translation is necessary—in fact, any translation seems impossible." Hans-Georg Gadamer, *Truth and Method*, Second, revised ed., translation revised by Joel Weinsheimer and Donald G. Marshall (New York: Continuum, 1993), 384–5.

14 Pyotr Ilyich Tchaikovsky, in Modeste Tchaikovsky, *The Life and Letters of Pyotr Ilyich Tchaikovsky*, ed. Rosa Newmarch (New York: John Lane Company, 1906), 280–1.

15 Stendhal, *The Life of Henry Brulard*, trans. John Sturrock (New York: The New York Review of Books, 2002), 201–3.

Wisdom

1 Aristotle, *Nicomachean Ethics*, 345 (translation modifed).

2 Aristotle said that Thales, who actually did fall into a ditch while looking at the stars, was wise (*sophos*) but not prudent (*phronimos*). Aristotle, *Nicomachean Ethics*, 345.

3 Henry G. Liddell, Robert Scott, and Henry S. Jones, *Greek-English Lexicon, Abridged Edition* (London: Oxford University Press, 1989), 643. See: http://stephanus.tlg.uci.edu/lsj/#eid=98436&context=lsj.

Writing as Meditation

1 Michel Foucault, *Remarks on Marx*, 27.

2 Diogenes Laertius, *Lives of Eminent Philosophers*, trans. R. D. Hicks (Cambridge, MA: Harvard University Press, 2006), 13.

3 Plato, *Euthyphro, Apology, Crito, Phaedo, Phaedrus*, trans. Harold North Fowler (Cambridge, MA: Harvard University Press, 1990), 83.

4 Saint Augustine, *Confessions*, trans. Henry Chadwick (New York: Oxford University Press, 1991), 145.

5 Hugh of St. Victor, *The Didascalion*, trans. Jerome Taylor (New York: Columbia University Press, 1991), 48.

6 Michel Foucault, *The Hermeneutics of the Subject*, ed. Frédéric Gros, trans. Graham Burchell (New York: Palgrave Macmillan, 2005), 15.

7 Plotinus, *The Enneads*, 54.

8 Musonius Rufus, *Stoic Fragments*, trans. Cora Lutz (New Delhi: Isha Books, 2013), 17–18.

9 Aristotle, *Nicomachean Ethics*, trans. H. Rackham (Cambridge, MA: Harvard University Press, 1994), 87 (translation modified).

10 Foucault, *The Hermeneutics of the Subject*, 416–17.

11 Foucault, *The Hermeneutics of the Subject*, 237.

12 Foucault, *The Hermeneutics of the Subject*, 356.

13 Foucault, *The Hermeneutics of the Subject*, 356–7.

14 Michel Foucault, "Writing the Self," in *Foucault and His Interlocutors*, ed. Arnold I. Davidson (Chicago, IL: University of Chicago, 1997), 236.

15 Foucault, in Davidson, *Foucault and His Interlocutors*, 240.

16 Plato, *Lysis, Symposium, Gorgias*, 93.

17 Marcel Proust, *Within a Budding Grove*, 605–6. Proust, *À l'ombre des jeunes filles en fleurs*, 427.

18 This is my own translation from the Greek text in Aeschylus, *Oresteia*, ed. and trans. Alan H. Sommerstein (Cambridge, MA: Harvard University Press, 2008), 20–1 (lines 176–183).

Demonstration

1 See Charles Darwin, *The Origin of Species*, ed. Gillian Beer (New York: Oxford, 1996), 3.

2 René Descartes, *Discourse on Method and Meditations on First Philosophy, Fourth Edition*, trans. Donald A. Cress (Indianapolis: Hackett Publishing Company, 1998), 19.

Interpretation

1 Martin Heidegger, *The Basic Problems of Phenomenology*, trans. Albert Hofstadter (Bloomington: Indiana University Press, 1988), 23.

2   Martin Heidegger, "The Origin of the Work of Art," in *Off the Beaten Track,* trans. Julian Young and Kenneth Haynes (New York: Cambridge University Press, 2002).

3   Hannah Arendt, *Between Past and Future* (New York: Penguin Books, 1993), 15.

4   Heidegger, *Being and Time,* 146.

5   Here I am indebted to Hans-Georg Gadamer. See Gadamer, *Truth and Method,* 300–7.

Perspective

1   See "Myth and Reality" in Simone de Beauvoir, *The Second Sex,* trans. H. M. Parshley (New York: Knopf, 1993), 267–80.

2   Friedrich Nietzsche, *On the Genealogy of Morality,* trans. Carol Diethe (New York: Cambridge University Press, 2002), 92 (translation modified). Nietzsche, *Zur Genealogie der Moral* (Frankfurt: Insel Verlag, 1991), 114.

3   Hans-Georg Gadamer described this movement of thought as a "fusion of horizons". See Gadamer, *Truth and Method,* 306.

Narration

1   On human existence as a project, see Heidegger, *Being and Time,* 140.

2   Charles Taylor, *Sources of the Self* (Cambridge, MA: Harvard University Press, 1989), 48 and 51.

3   On humans as "thrown" into the world, see Augustine, *Confessions,* 18, and Heidegger, *Being and Time,* 127.

Dialogues

1 Augustine, quoted in Karl Jaspers, *Plato and Augustine,* trans. Ralph Manheim (New York: Harcourt Brace & Company, 1962), 77. For the quotation in context, see Augustine, *Against the Epistle of Manichaeus, Called Fundamental,* trans. Rev. Richard Stothert (Savage, MN: Lighthouse Christian Publishing, 2017), 3.

2 Iris Murdoch's dialogues are exemplary in this respect. See Murdoch, *Acastos* (New York: Viking, 1987).

3 René Girard, *Job the Victim of his People,* trans. Yvonne Freccero (Stanford, CA: Stanford University Press, 1987), 32.

4 Tracy, *Plurality and Ambiguity,* 28.

Stories

1 Hannah Arendt, *Men in Dark Times* (New York: Harcourt Brace & Company, 1995).

2 My thoughts on narrative are deeply indebted to Michael Arndt. See his videos on storytelling on YouTube or at www.pandemoniuminc.com.

3 Here I am deeply indebted to Marshall Ganz. See his worksheet, "Telling Your Public Story" at https://www.scribd.com/document/551088014/Public-Story-Worksheet07Ganz.

4 Charles Taylor, *Philosophical Arguments* (Cambridge, MA: Harvard University Press, 1997), 53 (italics added).

5 George Saunders, *A Swim in a Pond in the Rain* (New York: Random House, 2021), 226–7.

6 Hannah Arendt most clearly laid out this argument—that in stories of human events, "causality . . . is an altogether alien and falsifying category." Arendt, *Essays in Understanding*, 319.

7 Heidegger, *Being and Time*, 113 and 115–16.

8 Milan Kundera, *The Art of the Novel*, trans. Linda Asher (New York: Harper & Row, 1993), 42.

9 Arendt laid out this argument in *The Human Condition*. "Who somebody is or was we can know only by knowing the story of which he is himself the hero." Arendt, *The Human Condition* (Chicago, IL: University of Chicago Press, 1989), 186.

10 Charles Taylor, *Sources of the Self* (Cambridge, MA: Harvard University Press, 1989), 33.

11 Leo Tolstoy, *A Confession and Other Religious Writings* (New York: Penguin Books, 1987), 22, 59, and 65.

12 Alasdair MacIntyre, *After Virtue, Third Edition* (Notre Dame, IN: University of Notre Dame Press, 2015), 219.

13 Epicurus, the Letter to Menoeceus, in Diogenes Laertius, *Lives of Eminent Philosophers, Volume II* (Cambridge, MA: Harvard University Press, 1931), 648–9 (translation modified).

Principles

1 H. L. Mencken in *Modern Essays on Writing and Style*, ed. Paul Charles Wermuth (New York: Holt, Rinehart, Winston, 1969), 17.

2 On how we acquire skills, see Hubert and Stuart Dreyfus, "From Socrates to Expert Systems," in *Skillful Coping* (New York: Oxford University Press, 2016), 25–46.

Process

1 Pierre Hadot, *The Inner Citadel*, trans. Michael Chase (Cambridge, MA: Harvard University Press, 2001), 51.

2 Seneca, *Letters on Ethics*, trans. Margaret Graver and A. A. Long (Chicago, IL: University of Chicago Press, 2015), 284.

3 Ernest Hemingway, *A Farewell to Arms,* "The Author's 1948 Introduction" (New York: Scribner, 1957), x.

Outline

1 Milan Kundera, *Testaments Betrayed,* trans. Linda Asher (New York: HarperPerennial, 1995), 172.

2 Epictetus, *Discourses, Fragments, Handbook,* 287.

3 Jean-Jacques Rousseau, *The Social Contract,* trans. Judith Masters (New York: St. Martin's Press, 1978), 46.

4 Karl Marx, *The Communist Manifesto* (New York: Verso, 1998), 34 (translation modified).

5 Virginia Woolf, *How Should One Read a Book?* (London: Laurence King Publishing, 2020).

6 Janet Malcolm, *the Journalist and the Murderer* (New York: Vintage Books, 1990), 3.

Argument

1 Aristotle, *Nicomachean Ethics,* 443–5 [1154a23-24; translation modified].

Questions

1 Plato, *Euthyphro, Apology, Crito, Phaedo, Phaedrus,* trans. Harold N. Fowler (Cambridge, MA: Harvard University Press, 1990), 445 [237c].

2 Milan Kundera, *The Unbearable Lightness of Being,* trans. Michael Henry Heim (New York: Harper & Row, 1987).

Paragraphs

1 William Strunk and E. B. White, *Elements of Style,* 4th ed. (New York: Longman, 1999), Table of Contents.

2 Leo Tolstoy, *War and Peace,* trans. Richard Pevear and Larissa Volokhonsky (New York: Vintage Books, 2008), 811.

3 Maurice Blanchot, *Le livre à venir* (Paris: Éditions Gallimard, 1959), 333–4. Maurice Blanchot, *The Book to Come,* trans. Charlotte Mandell (Stanford, CA: Stanford University Press, 2003), 245 (translation modified).

Sentences

1 Plato, *Lysis, Symposium, Gorgias,* 267, (translation modified).

2 Homer, *The Iliad,* trans. Richmond Lattimore (Chicago, IL: University of Chicago, 1962), 125 (Book IV, lines 412–413) (translation modified).

3 Homer, *The Odyssey,* trans. Emily Wilson (New York: Norton, 2018), 493.

4 Fyodor Dostoyevsky, *The Brothers Karamazov,* trans. Richard Pevear and Larissa Volokhonsky (New York: Knopf, 1992), 657.

5 https://www.theguardian.com/books/1999/dec/24/news.

Words

1 Heidegger, *Being and Time*, 202 (translation modified).

2 Hannah Arendt, *On Violence* (New York: Harcourt Brace & Company, 1970), 43.

3 Immanuel Kant, letter of August 7, 1783. Cited by Hannah Arendt in Lectures on *Kant's Political Philosophy*, ed. Ronald Beiner (Chicago, IL: University of Chicago Press, 1989), 39.

INDEX

Aeschylus   72, 85, 102, 103
aesthetics   37–40, 60, 61, 182–5
Agamben, Giorgio
   on aesthetics and art   40
agathos/ἀγαθός   26–7, 52, 86
agnosticism   51, 52
aischros/αἰσχρός   40–2, 45
aletheia/ἀλήθεια   17–21, 45, 50, 59, 87, 92
allegory of the cave   92, 122
Anzaldúa, Gloria   6
Aquinas, Thomas   18
Arendt, Hannah
   on stories   107
   as an interpretive thinker   83
   on writing   5
argument   11, 12, 66, 77, 95, 97, 104, 115, 145–9
   by allusion   145
Aristotle   147–8
   Eudemian Ethics   41
   on meditation   66–7
   Nicomachean Ethics   62
askesis   66, 69
atheism   51, 52
Augustine   17–18, 66, 101
   Confessions   115
Aurelius, Marcus
   on beauty and goodness   41
   Meditations   135–6

Baumgarten, Alexander
   on aesthetics   37–8
beauty   20, 23, 24, 35, 37–46, 61, 70, 101, 183–5
   aesthetic views of   37–40, 45, 60, 62, 182
   kallistic view of (*see kalos*/καλός)
   ontological view of   37, 39
Blanchot, Maurice
   parallel topic sentences in   162–3
   on writing for oneself   33
Book of Job   104–5

Carson, Rachel
   on writing for oneself   32
communication   3, 6, 7, 30–1, 39, 59, 69, 183
composition   4, 11, 32, 54, 141, 159, 182
concise and verbose writing   138–9
conversation   4, 8, 18, 32–4, 55, 105, 112
counterexamples   155–6

Dante   122
Darwin, Charles   141
   as an inductive thinker   77

de Beauvoir, Simone   85
   as a perspectival thinker   85
demonstrative thought   11, 75,
      77–9, 95, 111, 161
   deduction   77
   induction   77–8
   reduction   78
Descartes, René
   as a reductive thinker   78
devotion   57, 60, 101, 135
dialogue   3, 12, 15, 30, 75, 87–8,
      96, 99, 101–5
   character and   101–2
   perspective and   101
   structure of   104
divinity   49, 51–3, 70
Dostoevsky, Fyodor
   Brothers Karamazov,
      The   171–2

Eliot, T. S.
   on writing for oneself   32
enumeration   147
Epictetus
   Handbook, The   143
   on writing   3–4
Epicurus
   on wisdom   125
epistemology   15–16, 60, 61,
      182–5
essays
   papers *versus*   97
   question-driven   97–9
   thesis-driven   99
ethics   22, 26–30, 32–5, 60–2,
      67, 69–71, 101, 102, 112,
      122, 149

   of writing for oneself   32–5
ethopoiein/ἠθοποιεῖν, *see*
   meditation
ethos/ἦθος, *see* ethics
examples   155–6

feedback   137–8
figurative language   177
Foucault, Michel
   on his own writing   5–6
   on writing as meditation   65–9

Gadamer, Hans-Georg   201 n.13
   on aesthetics and art   40
Girard, René   104–5
goodness   22–35, 39, 45, 60, 61,
      69–70, 101, 121, 122, 182–5
   ethical view of (*see*
      agathos/ἀγαθός)
   hedonic view of   24, 26
   instrumental view of   25, 26
   moral view of   25–8
   technical view of   24–6
Gorgias   165

Hadot, Pierre
   on writing as a spiritual
      exercise   135
Harries, Karsten
   on aesthetics and art   40
Hauerwas, Stanley   8–9
Hegel, Georg Wilhelm Friedrich
   on beauty   37
Heidegger, Martin
   Being and Time   30, 83, 118
   on interpretation   82
   "Letter on Humanism"   12

"Origin of the Work of Art,
   The" 82–3
Hemingway, Ernest
   Farewell to Arms, A 137
Hermeneutic phenomenology,
   tasks of
   Destruktion 82
   Konstruktion 82
   Reduktion 82
Hesiod
   on inspiration 48
Homer
   Iliad, The 42, 170
   on inspiration 48
   Odyssey, The 18–20, 170
   on perspective 86
horizon 33, 87, 112, 113, 118
   expansion of 88
   as limit of understanding 84
Hugh of St. Victor 66

ignorance 8, 111, 113, 151, 176
inspiration 47–57, 60, 70, 71
   Hesiod on 48
   Mendeleev on 48
   Nietzsche on 49–53
   Plato on 47, 53
   Shelley on 48
   Stendhal on 56
   Tchaikovsky on 53–4
interpretive thought 12, 81–4
   critique of ideology 81
   exegesis 81
   hermeneutic
      phenomenology 82

jargon 146, 173, 178

Jefferson, Thomas
   Declaration of
      Independence 77
Joyce, James 18
justice 28, 29, 61, 62, 85, 102,
   103, 124, 125, 148–9, 157

kalos/καλός 40–2, 45, 52, 60,
   121
Kant, Immanuel 179
Kaufmann, Walter 8
King, Martin Luther, Jr.
   "I Have a Dream" 168
knowledge 8, 12, 30, 37, 61, 63,
   69, 70, 75, 87, 91, 97, 123,
   153, 182–4
   as justified true belief 11
   scientific 62
   self-knowledge 116
   and understanding 15–16
Kundera, Milan
   on narration 119
   on the organization of a
      work 141
   on questions 151

language 6–9, 27, 29–31, 52, 59,
   62, 68–71, 88, 102
lethe/λήθη 19, 20
life stories 116
Lincoln, Abraham
   Gettysburg Address, The 161

MacIntyre, Alasdair 122–3
Malcolm, Janet
   *Journalist and the Murderer,
      The* 144

Marion, Jean-Luc   16
Marx, Karl
   Communist Manifesto   81–2, 144
meaning   12, 40, 51, 53, 68, 71, 81, 85, 91, 107, 116, 118–22, 153, 163, 169
meditation   6, 33–5, 65–72, 124, 135
   ancient *vs.* modern concept of   67
   as *ethopoiein*/ἠθοποιεῖν   67
Mencken, H. L.   129
Mendeleev, Dmitri   48
metaphors   176–7
morality   27, 28, 37, 86
moral philosophy   27–8, 60, 61, 183
Morrison, Toni   3
multiple drafts, writing   137
mythology   16

narrative thought   12, 89–92, 111, 116
   life stories   112
   public stories   108
   testimony   107–8
   transition stories   111–15
New Testament   86
Nietzsche, Friedrich
   on beauty   41, 44
   Genealogy of Morals, The   86
   on goodness   23, 33
   on inspiration   49–53
   on perspective   86–7
   on writing and thinking   4

order of a text   141–2
outlines   141–4

papers   95–6
   essays *versus*   97
   thesis-driven   95, 99
paragraphs   143, 159–63
perspectival thought   12, 85–8
   demythification   85
   dialogue   85
   genealogy   85–6
phenomenology   176
   Hermeneutic   82
philosophy   15, 65–7, 125, 175, 185
   ancient   67
   moral   27–8, 60, 61, 182–4
Plato
   allegory of the cave   92, 122
   on beauty   41, 45
   Crito   103
   on dialogue   101
   on inspiration   47–8
   Phaedrus   45, 47, 52–3
   on wisdom   60–1
Plotinus
   on beauty   37
Plutarch   67, 69
principles   69, 129–33
process   135–40
proofreading   139–40
Proust, Marcel   55
   on involuntary memory   107
   on narration   92
   In Search of Lost Time   115
   on reading as revelation   20

on style 22
on wisdom 71
as a writer of very long sentences 166, 167
on writing for oneself 33–4
public stories
call to action 109
personal story 108–9
personal story in larger history 109
political discourse 111
structure of 110
Pythagoras 65

questions 22, 60, 97–9, 102–4, 113, 181–3, 185
topic introduction by 151–2
quotations 157–8

reading
as accompaniment to writing 136
as revelation 20
relevance 146–7
ressentiment 43–4
revelation 16–18, 21, 22, 49, 50, 70, 87, 88, 113, 115
Ricoeur, Paul 16
on morality and ethics 27
Rilke, Rainer Maria 21
Rousseau, Jean-Jacques
Social Contract, The 144
Rufus, Musonius 66

Saunders, George 16
Scheler, Max
strangely beautiful writing of 43–4
scientism 12, 59, 62, 77–9, 91, 141
self
as being in the world 118–20
as object of knowledge 116–17
as project 120–1
as subject 117–18
self-expression 3, 6, 57, 59, 69, 183
Seneca
on reading and writing 136
sentences 16, 143, 157–63, 165–73
complex 166–8
concise 165
emphatic words of 169
extended compound subjects, avoiding 172–3
parallel structures 168
related works 169
simple 165
Shelley, Percy Bysshe
on inspiration 48
Socrates 3, 47, 60, 61, 66, 103, 151
Symposium 70
sophia/σοφία, *see* wisdom
spirituality 66
Stendhal
on work and inspiration 56
stories 12, 13, 15, 27, 44, 71, 90–2, 107–25, 149
life stories 115, 116, 123, 124
public 108–11
testimony 107–8

transition 111–17
Strunk, William 159
style 4, 22, 42–4, 46, 60, 129, 136, 145, 167

Taylor, Charles 15
   on morality 27–8
   on narration 89
   on self 121
   on stories 115
Tchaikovsky, Pyotr
   on inspiration 53–4
testimony 107–8
theism 51, 52
thinking 3–5, 8, 9, 11–13, 22, 28, 65, 68, 75, 107, 151, 155, 156, 175, 184
   critical 12–13
   demonstrative 11, 77–9
   interpretive 12, 81–4
   narrative 12, 92, 115
   perspectival 12, 85, 87, 88
   scientistic 12
Thoreau, Henry David 42–3
Tolstoy, Leo
   Anna Karenina 137
   Confession, A 115, 121–2
   Death of Ivan Ilyich, The 115
   War and Peace 160–1
Tracy, David 18, 105
transition stories 111–17
truth 8, 11, 13, 15–22, 24, 33–5, 45, 46, 50, 60, 61, 66, 69, 72, 87, 97, 101, 113, 115–18, 123–5, 138, 162, 181, 183–5
   as correspondence 15–17, 21, 59, 92
   as illumination 18, 105
   (*see also aletheia/ἀλήθεια*)
   in others views, grains of 147–8

ugliness, *see aischros/αἰσχρός*
understanding 5, 6, 12, 13, 15, 16, 18, 21, 22, 26–8, 33, 39, 40, 45, 50–3, 57, 66, 68–72, 78, 79, 81, 83, 84, 86, 89–92, 97–9, 102, 111, 113, 114, 117, 118, 122–5, 135, 137, 172, 181, 183, 184
   authentic and inauthentic 8, 119, 120
   average and genuine 7, 8, 119, 145, 146
   common 7, 69, 119, 175
   limited 7
untruth, *see lethe/λήθη*

van Gogh, Vincent 83
verbs
   active and passive 169–72
   into nouns, avoid turning 177–8
virtues 24, 27, 41, 42–6, 60–3, 70, 71, 86, 96, 124, 179

White, E. B. 159
Wiesel, Elie
   Night 137
Williams, Bernard
   on morality 28

wisdom 57, 59–63, 65–6, 68, 70–2, 101, 107, 115, 116, 123–5, 129, 136, 184, 185
Woolf, Virginia 144
words 4, 13, 15, 19, 20, 26, 29, 52, 90, 160, 169, 175–9
  precise 175
  simplest appropriate 175
  technical 176
world 3, 6, 7, 13, 20–2, 27, 28, 30–2, 37, 47, 52, 53, 69–71, 81, 83, 84, 88, 89–92, 97, 101, 112, 118, 119, 122, 124, 129, 170, 172

Zinsser, William 8